HOPE FOR WOUNDED HEARTS

TRUE STORIES TO STRENGTHEN YOUR WEARY SOUL

CHRISTIAN WRITERS FOR LIFE

CONTENTS

Introduction	vii
1. Why, God? By Patricia "Trish" Kanipe	1
2. I Lost My Hero, I Found My Father By Luz Reyes	5
3. Discovering Life Beyond Abuse By Yolisa Mapisa	9
4. Freedom Found in Forgiveness By Tina White	13
5. Hurt to Hope By Lynda Juda	17
6. Through The Deep, Turbulent Waters By Kelly Jeanne	21
7. 'Til The Storm Passes By By Reba Whitley	25
8. The Invisible Shield By Rosemary Osborne	29
9. On the Wings of an Angel By Pamela Jannarone Scott	33
10. A Great Day to Die By Brent Clark	37
11. Not On My Watch By Jane N. Geiger	41
12. God Heals the Brokenhearted By Linda Marie	47
13. God Changed My Direction By Mollie Astromowicz	51
14. The Promise By Donna Bolk	55
15. The Balm of Gilead By Lynne Drysdale Patterson	59
16. There Is Hope in Jesus By Jacie Conley	63
17. A Chance to Forgive By Kelli Vasso	67

18. The Blues   71
By Sharon Kirby
19. Out of the Darkness   75
By Pam Waddell
20. The Promise of a Rainbow   79
By Melissa Brown
21. Kevin's Story   83
By Ellen Kolman
22. Trusting in the Dark   87
By Joyce Farinella
23. It's Too Much!   91
By Sandy Alsworth
24. The Garment of Praise   95
By Marcey Stevens
25. Healing from Workplace Trauma   99
By B. Anne Stevens
26. Knocked Down, but Not Knocked Out   103
By Mel Tavares
27. Forgiveness and Opportunity   107
By Susan King
28. The Nurse in Blue Scrubs   111
By Tammy Moser
29. Change Required   115
By Phil Bray
30. Walking by Faith   119
By Jane Reese
31. Cinnamon and Apples No More   123
By Sara Thornburgh
32. Love Takes No Account of the Wrong Done to It   127
By Rebecca A. Owens
33. Liquid Sunshine   131
By Carol V. Meyer
34. Confronting Cancer with Hope   135
By Lana Wynn Scroggins
35. Survivor   139
By Rose Walker
36. The Redemption of Even the Most Difficult Dates   143
By Loral Pepoon
37. Faithful Love   147
By Debbie Phillips
38. Hope Found in Our Wonderful Counselor   151
By Tony Farinella

39. Love Lifted Me — 155
By Judy Davis
40. Light in the Darkness — 159
By Tommye Lambert
41. Breaking Free — 163
By Desiree Hull
42. His Gifts from the Sea — 167
By Gayle Childress Greene
43. Burden Bearers — 171
By Norma Walters
44. In His Hand — 175
By Flora Reigada
45. Breathe — 179
By Kathy Stephens Bowen
46. Restored for More — 183
By Abigail Rayn
47. Hope Comes in Healing — 187
By Susan Shumway
48. My Last Day? — 191
By Susan Berg Heeg
49. My Duck of Grace — 195
By Susan Stedman
50. He's on Time — 199
By Janet Shearer
51. Hope Overcomes Grief — 203
By Dianne J. Richardson
52. The Promise — 207
By Lisa A. DeNunzio-Gomes
53. My Angel Wears Pearls — 211
By Teresa Newton-Terres
54. Three Layers of Grief — 215
By Rhonda Moore
55. A Poinsettia for Christmas — 219
By Sharon Rose Gibson
56. Courage to Live a Meaningful Life — 223
By Andy Bui

INTRODUCTION

Hope for Wounded Hearts: True Stories to Strengthen Your Weary Soul, is a collection of true stories that traverse the deep valleys and climb the steep inclines of human experience. Within these pages, you'll find the pain of loss, the struggle against unbeatable odds, and the grief, despair, and doubt found within personal and family crises.

Each story reaffirms the enduring strength of faith in God, the unbreakable bonds of family and friends, and the healing power of church and community. As you read these stories, you may see reflections of your own struggles, and, with God's help, perhaps discover new ways to navigate your path forward.

May these heartfelt stories invite you to engage deeply, reflect personally, and emerge with a renewed sense of God's love and care, purpose and faith. These writers remind us that although our hearts may be wounded, God is the wellspring of heart-healing and hope. These stories also reassure us that we are never alone in our suffering, that God stays close to us, giving us divine strength to comfort our weary souls.

1

WHY, GOD?

BY PATRICIA "TRISH" KANIPE

I have never met a victim of trauma who didn't eventually come clean and ask, "Where were you, God?" Jesus asked the same question when on the cross.

That question hindered my healing and spawned many dangerous emotions. I wallowed in Psalm 142:4—"I looked to my right and saw no one is concerned for me. I have no refuge; no one cares for my soul." The modern version might be, "Nobody loves me, everybody hates me … I'm gonna go eat worms!" I've never tasted a worm, but Satan's propaganda and the pain of bondage remained.

I struggled to hide the deep-seated conflict in my heart. I was sure that God would be angry if I openly expressed my thoughts and emotions. I blamed God for Satan's cruelty and sulked in bitterness. It is crucial that we deal with feelings, grieve, and take time to heal, but there is a potential danger lurking in the process. If we linger long, we can unwittingly become captive to Satan's lies and wallow like pigs in sludge.

So, how do you free yourself from the pigsty? It's a challenging practice of learning to surrender your thoughts to God instead of yourself and Satan's open door. Your thoughts control your beliefs, and your beliefs control every aspect of your life. Garbage in, garbage out!

There were two passages fundamental to my healing. Second Corinthians 10:5-6 was my first instruction from God: "We demolish arguments and every pretension that sets itself up against the knowledge of God, and we take *every* thought captive to make it obedient to Christ."

Learning to take thoughts captive was like trying to walk on water. I experienced countless failures until I earnestly applied Philippians 4:4-9. I learned to examine every gloom-ridden emotion using the lens of God's Word. Once you can manage your thoughts, your eyes will be opened to the truth that trauma wasn't sent from God.

Genesis 50:20 clearly states, "What Satan meant for evil, God meant it for good!" God didn't author the trauma or your pain, but He will use it. For much of my life, I dwelled in the cesspool of *Why?* But when God changed my thought process, He gave me two things: peace and purpose. Do you yearn for the same?

Your battles may feel overwhelming, but God is greater than all your doubts and struggles. True, everlasting healing can only be accomplished His way. I encourage you to take the first step and memorize 2 Corinthians 10:5-6 and Philippians 4:4-9. God's Word is the healer of our souls, and He greatly desires that you walk in His freedom. You merely need to take Him up on His promise.

* * *

Patricia "Trish" Kanipe is a believer, missionary, public speaker, survivor, and artist living in Boone, North Carolina. She studied education and psychology and is passionate about missions and teaching the "how-tos" of healing from trauma.

Questions for Personal Reflection or Group Discussion

Patricia "Trish" Kanipe delves into the spiritual and emotional turmoil of grappling with the aftermath of trauma. She shares her struggle with questioning God's presence during her suffering, feeling abandoned by God. The story highlights the power of Scripture in transforming one's mindset and seeing that trauma is not God-sent but can be used by God for greater purposes. Embracing this perspective helped Trish to move from a state of bitterness to one of peace and purpose.

Here are a few questions for personal reflection or group discussion:

1. Have you ever found yourself asking "Where were you, God?" during times of hardship? How did you reconcile or deal with these feelings?
2. What roles does Scripture play in your healing process? Ponder specific passages that have helped you through tough times.
3. What practical steps can you take to "take every thought captive to make it obedient to Christ"? How can this practice change your life?

2

I LOST MY HERO, I FOUND MY FATHER

BY LUZ REYES

My world fell apart at the tender age of four. I could not wait for my father to come home from work. It was such a great feeling, jumping into his loving arms for a strong and warm embrace. My dad was my hero. But that suddenly ended, and my life changed forever.

My dad was a police officer, and early one morning, on his way to work, a car driven by a drunk driver crashed his motorcycle and killed him. He was only twenty-nine years old, leaving behind a wife and six children.

A couple members of the police department arrived at our door with sad expressions on their faces to give my mom the devastating news. I remember my mom crying, and I know how hard it must have been for her to share the devastating news with my siblings and me.

The days that followed were very dark for me. I missed my dad tremendously. There was a trial regarding the accident, and one day, I went with mom to court. I remember a man bringing out a cardboard box from the back room. He reached into the box and pulled out the tattered uniform my dad was wearing that day. I could not hold back the warm tears. That scene remained in my memory. No matter how I acted and appeared on the outside, I was incredibly sad and empty on the inside.

To whom do you turn to when your world falls apart? As I sat on the porch, I remember looking up at the sky and talking to God about how I was feeling. On that day, I expressed to Him my feelings of hurt, loneliness, and emptiness. I said to God that from that day forward, I would turn to Him as my Father.

He has never failed me. I am very blessed to know that no matter what comes my way, I have a Heavenly Father who cares about every situation in my life—someone I can trust who will protect and never leave me.

"The Lord himself goes before you and will be with you; He will never leave you nor forsake you. Do not be afraid; do not be discouraged" (Deuteronomy 31:8). This Scripture became so real to me. I know that I am in His care, and that everything will turn out all right. I lost my hero; however, I found my Heavenly Father.

Whatever you are going through, know that there is a Heavenly Father who is there with and for you. You can always turn to Him. He is the healer.

"He heals the brokenhearted and binds up their wounds" (Psalm 147:3).

* * *

Luz Reyes is one of seven children, mom to three adult children, and grandmother to three amazing grandchildren. Born in Puerto Rico and now residing in Connecticut, Luz enjoys reading, writing, and walking on the beach.

Questions for Personal Reflection or Group Discussion

When Luz Reyes's policeman father died in a tragic accident, Luz's young world stopped. As a child, Luz grappled with intense feelings of sadness and loneliness. She found solace in speaking to God and seeking a new kind of paternal support from her Heavenly Father. This spiritual journey fortified the child's resilience. She embraced the comforting verses of the Bible and found hope in God's eternal care and love.

Here are a few questions for personal reflection or group discussion:

1. In times of profound grief, to whom do you turn for comfort, and why?
2. Ponder how tangible reminders, like Luz's father's uniform, can affect the grieving process.
3. Luz draws strength from God's Word. What Bible passages have given you the most comfort during difficult times in your life?

3

DISCOVERING LIFE BEYOND ABUSE

BY YOLISA MAPISA

"I do not claim that I have already succeeded or have already become perfect; I keep striving to win the prize for which Christ Jesus has already won me to Himself. Of course, my brothers, I do not think that I have already won it. The one thing I do, however, is to forget about what is behind me and to reach what is ahead of me."
(Philippians 3:12-13)

I was sexually abused at the age of five, and this experience convinced me that, even as a young girl, my life was a dead end. I felt confused and utterly astonished at the cruelty of humankind. I felt like I lived in a small, dark cage. Darkness, anger, and confusion filled my little mind for so many years that I couldn't see any beauty in life, or in me.

As I grew, I couldn't work very well with people, and men became my primary targets. When I looked at them, I only saw cannibals.

At school, I became quiet, looking down on myself while

wanting to make sure that I did better than the boys. I was miserable, and my life was a mess.

History has a way of repeating itself, and when I thought I had finally come to terms with what happened to me at age five, the worst happened again when, as I reached the age of sixteen, my uncle assaulted me twice. When he wanted to do it a third time, I threatened to tell my mother, so he stopped.

I couldn't understand why God allowed those things to happen to me, and I became bitter toward Him. I tried to figure out a life outside the pain and confusion I was feeling, and the only way to do that was to use what I loved doing.

Music was my passion, and I had to find a way to use my talent to cover the misery I was in. I joined a church because I wanted to be able to find pleasure in life and to move on and forgive the people who had hurt me.

But again, the worst happened. A year after joining the church, one of the church leaders wanted to marry me by force, and he raped me with the intention of making me his wife.

I couldn't take it anymore, so I gave up. For two years, my life was almost destroyed. Finally, though, I made the decision to give my life to God completely and become actively involved in ministry. In doing this, God restored me completely and made me realize that there is life beyond sexual molestation.

Any journey requires determination, courage, and perseverance. As a determined victor, I needed to learn to work with people of different characters and personalities. I had to stand up above the circumstances and be ready to fight for my victory.

Through my horrific experiences with sexual assault, I learned that there's nothing I can do with my own power, but that I can give everything to God. He made me fearfully and wonderfully, and He'll make sure that I stay complete at all times. This knowledge gave me courage to appreciate the awesome creativity that God made.

* * *

Yolisa Mapisa is an alumna of Creare Ministries International where she studied drama, music, and writing. She dedicates her spare time to volunteering at an orphanage, and she writes short stories for children's skits.

Questions for Personal Reflection or Group Discussion

In this story, Yolisa Mapisa shares her painful past of bad experiences, traumas, and sexual abuse. Despite the overwhelming challenges, she finds strength and healing through her faith and is able to focus on the future, not her past pain, to define her.

Here are a few questions for personal reflection or group discussion:

1. How can focusing on the future rather than dwelling on past hardships help in personal healing?
2. Ponder the importance of community, faith, and professional help in the process of healing from traumas. Have you ever experienced a trauma after which community, faith, and professional help brought you healing? If so, reflect on that experience.
3. Reflect on how music and ministry can play a role in a person's recovery and redirection of life. How can hobbies, passions, and a sense of purpose help in overcoming past abuses?

4

FREEDOM FOUND IN FORGIVENESS

BY TINA WHITE

The darkness threatened to envelop me, as once again I woke up sweating and crying. Another night of night terror had disrupted my sleep.

Will this ever end? I cried out to God.

From the time I was six years old until I left home at age nineteen, I was sexually, physically, emotionally, mentally, verbally, and financially abused by my mother's then common-law husband.

Due to the severity of the abuse, I endured years of severe depression, anxiety, night terrors, and post-traumatic stress disorder.

For years, I blamed myself for the abuse. I hated myself and detested my abuser. I truly wanted him dead and for him to feel as much pain as he had caused me. But after years of struggling with all this unforgiveness God helped me to forgive myself and to forgive my abuser.

God placed me into a church who loved me until I could love myself. They taught me through their actions about unconditional love I had never felt or known before.

I also found a Christian counselor who worked with me. She

explained that forgiveness isn't for the other person, but rather it's for me. By forgiving my abuser and forgiving myself, I released myself from the prison I had been living in for over thirty-five years. I'm no longer allowing my abuser to control me any longer, and I'm getting my power back.

I knew I had fully forgiven myself and my abuser when the memories of my past no longer haunted me. I was no longer walking around angry all the time. I could sleep without having constant, night after night, night terrors.

Forgiveness isn't necessarily easy, but with God's help it is possible. I had to pray and ask God for His help to forgive my abuser. God did help me, through His forgiveness for me.

Today, my life is amazing. I have a peace of mind that I never knew was possible. The phenomenal joy I've been able to attain today has only come from God and a lot of hard work in counseling. I no longer have bad days; I may have a bad moment, but not an entirely bad day anymore.

Through God's unconditional He has for me, and through His telling me how worthy I am, today I can honestly say I truly love myself.

If you are struggling with unforgiveness, remember the forgiveness is for you, so that you can be set free, not for the other person. When you forgive, unforgiveness will no longer control you, and you will gain your freedom and take your power back.

* * *

Tina White is a daughter, sister, aunt, and author. She has published two books, *Renewed Gem: A Daughter of the King* and *Think on These Things: Self-Empowerment Prompts Journal for Christians by Queen Tamar*, both available on Amazon.

Questions for Personal Reflection or Group Discussion

This narrative tells the story of Tina White who suffered extensive abuse from a young age at the hands of her mother's common-law husband. The abuse proved sexual, physical, emotional, mental, verbal, and financial. This abuse led Tina to severe depression, anxiety, night terrors, and PTSD, haunting her well into adulthood. The turning point came when Tina found support in a loving church community and sought help from a Christian counselor who emphasized the healing power of forgiveness—not for the abuser, but for Tina herself.

Here are a few questions for personal reflection or group discussion:

1. Reflect on a time when forgiving someone had a profound impact on your emotional or mental well-being. How did this act of forgiveness change your outlook or circumstances?
2. How important are support systems, such as a church, community, or counseling, in overcoming past traumas? Share experiences where such support has been crucial in your own life.
3. How can faith in God play a role in personal transformation, especially in the context of recovering from abuse?

5

HURT TO HOPE

BY LYNDA JUDA

*S*trolling along down the sidewalk before supper, I looked for someone to play with. I crossed the street, and a few yards ahead, I could see a little girl about my age of seven playing on the sidewalk.

I approached her and asked if I could play with her, but she didn't answer. I sat down and began to play in the dirt with some sticks and rocks, forming them into numbers and pictures. Again, I asked the girl what her name was, but she didn't speak, so I continued to play.

All of a sudden, I felt something hard hit my head. The little girl had hit me with a brick. Just then, a woman came running from the house and demanded, "How did you get out?" Then the lady looked at me with a frightened look on her face. She grabbed the little girl's hand and dragged her to the house.

All I could think of was what the woman asked, "How dd you get out?" Did they have her chained up? It was time to go home.

As I stood up, I felt dizzy, but I managed to stagger home. When I opened the door, my mother yelled, "Lynda!"

I wondered, *Am I that late for supper?*

My mother said, "Your hair is full of blood!" I put my hand on my head, and I could feel the cold, sticky blood.

Minutes later, my mother called the police, and we met the policeman outside.

"Show me the house," my mother said. "Stay here." She and the policeman went and knocked on the door. My mother was saying words I couldn't hear, but I'm sure the woman did. The policeman stayed at the house, and I went to the doctor and got eight stitches.

My head hurt for days, but I kept thinking of the little girl. I would pass her house as I walked to school, but I never saw her again. I was told a few days later that the little girl now had a new home. She was in a hospital especially for children like herself.

Isaiah 55 says His ways are far above our ways. I know now that what happened that day was God's plan. Sometimes I think that maybe some good came out of getting hit by a brick. I know it did. If I hadn't played with that little girl, she probably would still be chained up, or being abused, and who knows what life she would have, if any.

Hurt turned into hope that day—hope that no matter what happens in my life, God is the Creator of everything, even if it takes getting hit with a brick.

* * *

Lynda Juda is an artist, writer, and teacher. Her story "The Tree That Almost Wasn't," the story of a true Christmas miracle, was printed in her local paper. Lynda writes about true life experiences.

Questions for Personal Reflection or Group Discussion

Lynda Juda begins her story citing a childhood incident when she was seven years old. Lynda encounters a silent girl of similar age and attempts to engage her in play. The girl violently hits Lynda with a brick, leading to a serious injury. Lynda returns home dazed and bleeding. The incident prompts a police intervention, and the results show that the girl suffered from neglect and abuse. The investigation brought about a positive change for the young girl.

Here are a few questions for personal reflection or group discussion:

1. Lynda sees the event as part of God's plan. How do you interpret the event?
2. Can you recall a personal experience where a negative event led to a positive outcome? Reflect on what happened.
3. How can traumatic events contribute to personal growth and needed help?

6

THROUGH THE DEEP, TURBULENT WATERS

BY KELLY JEANNE

While my dad and siblings stood in a small circle, tossing a ball around, my mom watched from the front porch. Being the black sheep of the family, I didn't join in. Even at age seven, I knew my place.

Without warning, a German shepherd ran into the yard, slamming his entire eighty pounds straight into me, knocking me on my stomach. At this point, I could only guess it was something large and hairy. Along with his wet tongue, his sharp teeth jabbed into my flesh, as if I were being tasted for the kill. In my little mind, I knew I was going to die.

Please don't kill me!

Without turning his head or making any effort to help, my dad absentmindedly shouted, "Roll yourself into a ball and keep rolling around!" The others seemed equally unconcerned.

In my panicked state, it was difficult to hear anything. I felt like a rag doll as the dog shoved me onto my back. That's when I caught a glimpse of my mom's eyes. They were devoid of emotion yet revealed a hint of expectation, as if she hoped the dog would make an end of me. Mercifully, everything soon faded to black.

Being raised by a narcissist and a pedophile meant things didn't improve for me. Life at home was a nightmare.

Decades before I was aware of the concept of accepting Christ, I always had my mind on the things of God and saw how He answered my silent, tearful pleas. When an unjust punishment appeared inevitable, I cried out to Him. Many times, through His mercy, the abuse was derailed.

"Are they not all ministering spirits, sent forth to minister for them who shall be heirs of salvation?" (Hebrews 1:140)

The ministering spirits are His angels whom He sends to provide protection and care, even to those who are not as yet, but soon will be, heirs of salvation.

It wasn't until years later, when I accepted Christ into my life, that I fully appreciated how He had protected me during an unstable period in my life.

It never gives Him joy to see any of us headed for eternal damnation when we leave this physical realm. For those who are still without Christ, He does His utmost to keep the lines of communication open, just as He did with me during my childhood. He is always working on ways to reach us. That's a powerful, eternal love.

Are you listening to the ways He's speaking to you? Keep listening. Eventually, you'll find Him as I did. He never gives up on you. Please don't give up on Him.

* * *

Hailing from San Diego with her tabby, Luna, **Kelly Jeanne** is blessed to have three of her stories published in devotional anthologies by Christian Writers for Life. She is so thankful and blessed.

Questions for Personal Reflection or Group Discussion

Kelly Jeanne opens her story describing a childhood memory where she felt alienated as the black sheep of the family. She witnesses indifference from family members during a traumatic incident, an attack by a German shepherd. The attack leaves Kelly feeling utterly abandoned and fearing for her life. Raised in a deeply dysfunctional family, characterized by narcissism and abuse, Kelly finds solace in God's intervention. Years later, after accepting Christ, Kelly fully appreciates these interventions as acts of God's protection during her tumultuous upbringing.

Here are a few questions for personal reflection or group discussion:

1. Have you ever experienced a moment in your life that you later recognized as a form of divine intervention or protection? If so, ponder the experience.
2. How can individuals like Kelly find strength and healing when growing up in a dysfunctional family?
3. In what ways do you believe God communicates with us, especially in times of need? How can we become more attuned to these messages?

7

'TIL THE STORM PASSES BY

BY REBA WHITLEY

During an ordinary day, my eight-year-old daughter, Hannah, and I were home alone. It had been raining, and the rain eventually became a nasty storm.

The storm caused an unexpected power outage, so Hannah and I gathered candles and distributed them throughout the house. My husband was working two hours from home with no means of communication.

The wind grew fierce. We went to look out the front door, but the force of the wind ripped the door out of my hand and slammed it violently into the wall behind it. Stunned, we stared out at the chaos happening before our eyes. We were shocked to see a huge oak tree yield its long branches as the winds bent them until they almost touched the ground. We hurriedly moved behind the door and pushed against the wind to shut and bolt it.

Sitting quietly, we listened to the angry winds and the heavy rain beat loudly on the metal roof of our historic house. Lightning flashed passed the windows and thunder clapped with cracking sounds followed by rumblings so loud and deep we could feel the vibrations through the house's foundation.

Our senses were overwhelmed as we prayed for God's protection.

We listened to the raging storm, until there was instant, unexpected silence. It was quiet as death. There was no wind, no rain, and the afternoon sky soon became darker than a solar eclipse.

Rushing to look outside, we noticed an eerie stillness—not a leaf moving, nor a puff of wind. A thought rushed through my brain: *Hold onto your britches, girl. This can't be good!* I quickly shut and bolted the door and we huddled together in the inside corner of our log room.

There, we sat in silence. Have you ever noticed how deafening total silence can be? Within seconds, an alarming rumble shook the ground, and the sound of a freight train, plunged through our house. That sound shot through my bones like a sledgehammer.

Too frightened to move, the verses in Psalm 91 came to my mind, and I prayed God's promises. Within minutes, the storm was over. We and our home were safe and unharmed. Later, I asked Hannah what was going through her mind during the storm. She said she was praying and knew that if it wasn't our time to go, we'd be protected; and if it was, that would be okay too. *Wisdom from the mouth of babes.*

If you're ever in a similar situation, turn to God and depend on His protection. As far as I know, Jesus is the only one who has ever talked to a storm—"Peace, be still"—and it listened!

* * *

Reba Whitley writes Christian fiction mystery/suspense and magazine articles, and she contributes to anthologies in hopes of encouraging her readers to have strong faith in God and to talk with Him often.

Questions for Personal Reflection or Group Discussion

Reba Whitley and her daughter experience a severe storm while alone at home. In response to the escalating chaos, they secure the house and retreat to the safety of an inner corner in their log room, praying for God's protection as the storm reaches its peak. The experience becomes a testament to their faith and resilience, and it highlights the power of prayer and trust in God's protection during life's storms.

Here are a few questions for personal reflection or group discussion:

1. Have you ever experienced a moment of intense fear like a severe storm? How did you cope with the situation?
2. Reba mentions Psalm 91 as a source of comfort during the storm. Are there particular Bible passages that you turn to for comfort in difficult times? How do they help?
3. How can the perspectives of children during crises teach us about handling fear and uncertainty? Think back on an example where a child's insight or reaction impacted your own faith.

8

THE INVISIBLE SHIELD

BY ROSEMARY OSBORNE

God is an invisible shield. He can be trusted to save you with gentleness.

I'm with my parents touring the zoo at eleven o'clock at night. The tiger lies stretched out, relaxing, its head against the glass wall.

How often is it realistic to be in close contact with a tiger? I think. I had heard of the "tiger eye," a polished stone with mesmerizing, gold-striped shimmers, and now I want to see it for myself.

I bend close to observe the tiger's eyes through the clear glass. The tiger's eyes rest, along with its perfectly striped body.

Momentarily, I see a flash of black moving in the tiger's eyes. *Perhaps the tiger is annoyed, or has an attitude, even strong feelings combined with some sequence of thought. Maybe the tiger is jealous.*

In an instant, the tiger rolls and poises on its powerful hind legs. The tiger rises to full height, leaping above my head, and as it springs it hits the glass with the full impact of its pounce. The glass shudders but holds. I see the tiger's white fluffy underbelly, the claws sliding down the glass, the tiger's mouth open, its spray of whiskers, its tongue curled back in a fierce snarl.

The alarm bells ring, and the tiger turns with a growl of confusion and slouches away, white-tipped ears flicking on its drooping head. Clearly this tiger is not pleased. But also, the tiger is calm, recognizing the invisible restraint of the glass shield. I am also calm, thankful for this transparent shield.

"Did that scare you?" Mother asks. "What on earth were you doing? Can you imagine if the glass had broken?"

"I admired this tiger so much. What amazing power in that animal. I saw the jealousy in the tiger's eyes just before it struck," I enthuse. Mother is silent.

When Dad hears of the experience, he shakes his head. "Most people would not live to tell what you have seen," Dad says.

If you're in a similar situation, having once admired someone who has coveted the blessing God provided to your family, maybe you were protected. The deception still hurts, and you know it's critical to move forward with care.

David said, "Thou hast also given me the shield of Thy salvation, and Thy gentleness hath made me great" (2 Samuel 22:36). In this verse David speaks about how God shields him and promotes him with a reset. Like David, I also found God's gentleness releasing me to be transparent with Him, to be safe with Him uplifting me. As you unravel the intricate details of this mystery, truth will come from above and bring healing.

***

Rosemary Osborne has long-held a fascination with creative writing, and she dreams of someday seeing her manuscripts in print. She hopes that, in the future, her books will inspire others to live amazing lives.

Questions for Personal Reflection or Group Discussion

When Rosemary Osborne visits a night zoo with her parents, she encounters a tiger separated from her by a glass barrier. The tiger, provoked, leaps at the glass. The glass serves as a transparent shield, protecting Rosemary from a potentially terrifying confrontation. She draws a parallel between the physical shield of the glass and the spiritual shield that God provides. Her story highlights the theme of divine protection in the face of life's potential dangers.

Here are a few questions for personal reflection or group discussion:

1. How does this image of a "transparent shield" of glass serve as a metaphor for God's protection in your own life?
2. Ponder a time when you felt threatened in some way yet experienced a sense of protection and safety.
3. Reflect on how personal experiences can sometimes deepen understanding or appreciation of spiritual texts. Have you ever had an experience that brought a new or deeper meaning to a familiar Scripture or spiritual teaching?

9

ON THE WINGS OF AN ANGEL

BY PAMELA JANNARONE SCOTT

The summer heat of August rose relentlessly. Going for a ride in my uncle's dune buggy, one he'd built himself, was a perfect way to cool off. His craftsmanship was exceptional for an Air Force veteran. We'd ride through sugar white sand trails lined with pine trees and wildflowers, tall oaks of shade, the sun streaking in between as if God were watching and protecting us.

Today was a perfect day to ride as planned. But the hours passed. The summer sun of August set down into the horizon. I was still waiting for his ride.

The phone never rang. It was not like him not to show up. It seemed as if this day stood still in time, like a still-life painting with an unexplainable communication.

I waited and waited. And like an hourglass, tiny grains of sand slipped through a narrow path in silence, into the opening of the other side.

Then the knock came on the door. We were informed he was never coming home again.

This day changed our lives forever. We learned of his fatal

accident and how he saved his friend's life for his own. His last words were, "I'm going out for one last ride."

Losing a loved one so suddenly is devastating. My spirit felt jolted and confused.

"Why?" I asked God.

He was my hero too, my mentor, a positive reinforcement in my life who gave me hope.

I was an adolescent at the time and filled with mixed emotions. I endured difficult lessons throughout life after his death, but I remember his faith in God, his positive outlook on life. With shattered dreams and broken wings, I held on to his heroic efforts, knowing God saved his soul.

We grieve because of the love we have for our cherished family members. It is how we show our love.

God had plans that day for my uncle's destination. And He has plans for each of us. God holds the keys as Sovereign over life and death.

He sends His angels to those in deep despair and sorrow, and He always stays close to the brokenhearted. We are truly blessed to have a closer connection with God, holding on to His promise of everlasting life.

Each new sunrise brings forth a new day to challenge our faith. It is the day that He has made. We must rejoice in it because one day, it will be our turn to ride on the wings of an angel and be with our loved ones for all eternity.

We must keep this faith that it is so, and will be done, because there is nothing new under the sun.

* * *

Pamela Jannarone Scott is an award-winning author in the Christian Writers for Life anthology *Experiencing God's Presence*. She adores her precious Georgia family who inspire her to write with God. She loves Jesus.

Questions for Personal Reflection or Group Discussion

Pamela Jannarone Scott recounts the tragic day her uncle died in a fatal accident as he tried to save his friend's life. Struggling with confusion and grief, Pamela grapples with her uncle's sudden loss, reflecting on his positive influence, strong faith, and heroic spirit. The story touches on themes of sudden loss, the pain of grief, and the enduring impact of a loved one's legacy.

Here are a few questions for personal reflection or group discussion:

1. How do you cope with the shock and immediate grief following the sudden loss of a loved one?
2. Reflect on a loved one who has passed away, and ponder the positive impacts this loved one had on your life. How do you honor the person's memory?
3. How does faith in God influence the grieving process? Think back on personal experiences or observations on how love for and trust in God can provide comfort in times of deep sorrow.

10

A GREAT DAY TO DIE

BY BRENT CLARK

"That's it," I said aloud. "Goodbye, cruel world. It's a great day to die."

Tears streamed down my face. I stood on a cliff overlooking Royal Palms Beach. The afternoon sun blazed on the Pacific Ocean below without a cloud in the sky. I looked over the edge, staring at the jagged rocks below. My body shuddered at the thought of the impact on my body as it hit the rocks below.

What caused a sixteen-year-old boy to consider suicide? Report cards came in the mail that weekend. My parents weren't pleased. They screamed at the top of their lungs and lectured me about the importance of grades every time report cards came. That certain weekend, my father snapped, slammed me against the wall, and hit me a few times. He even spit at my feet when he was done.

"Spit on your mother and father!" he growled.

My father was twice my size. I was underdeveloped, a tall and skinny kid. This put a target on my back. I tried to put on size and strength by joining the football team, but the coaches wondered what I was doing on the football field. My teammates would crush me and mock me at the same time. Girls? Nobody wanted me. One girl even told me, "You're better off dead!" A few hours later I was on the cliff.

I was ready to meet the bitter end, no question about that. The question was, what was going to happen to me after I died? A friend of mine had told me about Jesus. He said that Jesus died for my sins and wanted to have a relationship with me. I didn't believe it because I never thought Jesus could want a loser like me. However, if I jumped, I knew I would die and go to Hell.

The realization that I had hit rock bottom hit me harder than any of the guys on the football team. Another realization even hit harder than that—I was self-destructive, and I needed Christ.

When I got back to my bedroom, I prayed that Jesus would rescue me from myself. I knew that if God didn't intervene, I might actually kill myself.

I'm now forty-nine years old. Jesus and His mercy and grace continue to cleanse me of my sin. That is the point of the gospel. The gospel points out that the human heart is sinful and self-destructive. Jesus Christ came and took out place for our sins on the cross. He rescues lost souls and changes their lives. Jesus never promised anyone an easy life, but He promised to be with us every step of the way.

* * *

Brent Clark is a writer and photographer living in Columbus, Ohio, with his wife, Tara, and their three dogs. He is a graduate of The Ohio State University with a B.A. in English.

Questions for Personal Reflection or Group Discussion

At age sixteen, Brent Clark stood on a cliff ready to end his life, overwhelmed by academic failures, parental abuse, and social rejection. In his darkest moment, he recalled a friend's words about Jesus' love and sacrifice, prompting him to reconsider his contemplation of suicide. He prays to God to rescue him from his self-destructive behavior. Later in life, Brent reflects on how his faith in Jesus guided and transformed him. The story highlights themes of despair, redemption, and the power of faith in life's challenges.

Here are a few questions for personal reflection or group discussion:

1. Reflect on how society and family expectations can impact a teen's mental health. Have you ever felt overwhelmed by such pressures? If so, how did you cope?
2. How were Brent's feelings of worthlessness and rejection transformed by God's divine love and forgiveness?
3. Brent later reflects on his life and the choices he made. How does reflecting on past struggles with the benefit of hindsight help us better understand and appreciate our growth and resilience?

11

NOT ON MY WATCH

BY JANE N. GEIGER

He broke my heart
When I told him I believed in
And loved Jesus
Would spend my life loving others
To Christ, to healing, blazing into their pain
With the healing balm of Gilead

He disowned me that day, barely sixteen
Not so sweet

He broke my heart
When he would never
Let me go on a church or
Youth group retreat
No fun for a teenager
Being the "freak"

"Not on my watch"

He broke my heart
When he said, "No"
To my Air Force Academy dreams
Just maybe, the Top of Top Gun

Patriot, protecting America's freedoms
Protecting Americans

Already accepted
Senators' letters inked
Practiced pressing precision for
Perfect dress blues, officer whites
Polishing brass
Practicing actually
Being polished

When he said, "No" this time …

I did not speak to him for months
Under the same high school roof of
My parents' house
Not my home
Homeless at home

He broke my heart when I quit
My secure money job
To found a nonprofit
In the urban section of town … risky
Too far from our suburban hills
He rejected me fiercely this time
Disappointment on his face, deep sadness in his soul

He never came to our opening
Never entered the Christian counseling practice
He sent faxes to my secretary
Describing my nonprofit "surely to fail"

Juxtaposed
Dad and Jesus
"Honor your Mother and Father, that it may go well with you
All the days of your life."
Caught in the crosshairs, I was

Dutiful Daughter
Respectful Relating
Perpetual Pain

He broke my heart
When he refused to attend, pay for
Or do anything with my church wedding
He withheld my mother that day
Excruciating, as he knew the key to breaking me
Was to withhold her, the Mother of the Bride
I broke like a porcelain doll thrown
On marble flooring
Shattered

I thought I would die that day

What he did not know
Was that this breaking of me
All of this human rejection by him
Accomplished precisely what God intended
Through the strong father of a strong-willed daughter:

Protection

I was spared assaults by a pedophile at youth retreats
I was never cornered in any barracks, no "General's Daughter"
Held down by men in military uniforms, circa 1988
No man assaulted my trusting soul, youthful body
Before I could hold my own against the strength of a male attacker

I broke my own heart
When I let him die without thanking him
For protecting me, fiercely so
This failure happened on my watch, he's not here to see the fruits of his labor …
I am his Healthy Grateful Daughter

May this NEVER happen to you on your watch
Are you watching?

* * *

Rev. Dr. Jane N. Geiger, M.A., is a counselor, author, speaker, mediator, and minister who lives to broker God's grace to all people as the founder and president of Grace Ministries, Inc. —www.WritersCupOfGrace.com.

Questions for Personal Reflection or Group Discussion

Jane N. Geiger's poetic story revolves around the complex and painful relationship between a daughter and her father, marked by repeated conflicts over her life choices and beliefs. Despite the father's harsh methods and seeming lack of support, Jane later recognizes that his strict restrictions potentially shielded her from serious harms, bringing a bittersweet perspective to her father's actions.

Here are a few questions for personal reflection or group discussion:

1. How can you maintain your own beliefs and values when they are in direct conflict with those of your family?
2. Reflect on a time when someone's actions hurt you but were intended to protect you. How did you come to understand the motivations, and how did this affect your relationship?
3. Ponder the importance of forgiveness and reconciliation, especially in family relationships. Reflect on a personal experience where you either extended forgiveness or wish you had.

12

GOD HEALS THE BROKENHEARTED

BY LINDA MARIE

When I was eighteen years old, I lost my dad to suicide. He was a bigger than life figure to me. He was a Navy pilot, tall, handsome, a gentleman, and one of the kindest people I have ever known. He was also a writer, and every time I sit down at the computer to write, I remember him sitting at the kitchen table with a legal pad of paper and pen in hand. He was only forty-six years old when he died. His death was the most painful thing I have ever been through.

I grew up in an age when suicide was considered to be an unforgivable sin. If someone died that way, they could not go to Heaven. Many years have passed, and after reading the Bible, I have found the only unforgivable sin listed is to blaspheme the Holy Spirit. With the love of friends and the experience of knowing and learning about God, I have come to terms with his passing. I now rest in the hope of seeing him in Heaven one day.

One friend explained that just like some people have a heart attack, when someone commits suicide, it is like having a brain attack. It is unpredictable. It is an illness and not a part of who they were as a person. I found this thought helpful.

When someone commits suicide, other people don't know

what to say or do. As a survivor, I appreciated every attempt by someone who tried to lessen my pain. As a friend of others who are suicide survivors, I too have struggled with what to say. We wonder how and why this happened. Some will ask those questions, but I have found many do not ask the most important questions—questions that open the door for the survivor to share what their loved one was like as a person.

One of the hardest parts of this type of death is that many times, the survivors don't get the chance to share what their loved one's *life* was like, what made them special, what they loved about them. When the time is right for the survivor to share, it is so important to have someone near who will listen with their whole heart.

I was fortunate. God sent a person after my father's death who listened and loved me through the initial stages of loss. And it is true that sometimes just having someone sit quietly as a praying presence is a great comfort.

Only God can truly heal a broken heart. The best that we can give to someone is to use our actions and prayers—our love—to help bring them closer to God.

* * *

Linda Marie is an Amazon author and illustrator of *Forty Footsteps* and *The Adventures of Cleo the Cloud*. She is a licensed cosmetologist and Stephen Minister with a certificate of Spiritual Direction/Theology from Spring Hill College.

Questions for Personal Reflection or Group Discussion

When Linda Marie was eighteen years old, her father committed suicide. It left a lasting mark of grief and confusion on Linda. This story underscores the importance of compassionate listening and the significant role of faith in God in healing a broken heart, reinforcing that while only God can mend such deep wounds, the love and support of others are invaluable in the path toward healing.

Here are a few questions for personal reflection or group discussion:

1. How does faith in God influence the grieving process, especially in coping with the loss of a loved one to suicide?
2. What are effective ways to support someone who has lost a loved one to suicide? Ponder the importance of listening and acknowledging the loved one's life beyond their manner of death.
3. Reflect on the statement, "Only God can truly heal a broken heart." How can individuals help guide those who are grieving toward finding comfort in God and His Word?

13

GOD CHANGED MY DIRECTION

BY MOLLIE ASTROMOWICZ

You have been put on academic probation until December 2023.

I had been so motivated to continue pursuing my bachelor's degree after receiving my associate's degree, yet there I was, reading the email that had just come through. I was struggling to keep a passing grade in my classes. I had lost all motivation to continue toward my degree. I was overwhelmed each time I logged in or even received an email from my college.

I ended the fall semester of 2022 with one barely passing grade and three failed classes. A few weeks later, I received that email that made my heart drop.

December 2023 was one year from the day that I read that email. I had no idea what to do with myself. It took me three months to even tell my parents what had occurred because I didn't know how to process that letter. After, I decided to take the time off to rest, recover, and work through that hard time with God. Where else could I turn but to Him?

As time went on, throughout my surprise break from college, I finally started feeling at peace again. I no longer felt stressed to check my email or worried about my grades as I went through my day. By the beginning of summer, I realized that this sudden break had been a gift from God.

He knew I wasn't entirely sure about starting the next degree immediately. I did it because my advisor told me I'd have to pay the admission fee again if I didn't continue right then. When the back-to-school season came around, I longed to return to college. However, according to the email, I couldn't re-enroll until the spring semester of the following year.

As everyone else was returning to college, I found myself looking into transferring to a Christian college. I called and asked the college about admissions, and while I was on the phone, I asked if I could transfer if I was on academic probation. They said I could, as long as my previous college wrote a letter removing the probation.

I called my old college the next day, and I was shocked to learn that they didn't even have the probation on file. In October of 2023, I started my first semester at my new Christian college.

As the Bible says in Romans 8:28, "We know that all things work together for the good of those who love God—those whom He has called according to His plan." What started as a huge tragedy soon became a clear pathway for the next step in my educational journey.

If you ever feel confused about your situation, just know that God holds the master plan.

*　*　*

Mollie Astromowicz is a golfer, teacher, writer, and auntie to eight who is living the New England life. She loves to hang out with family and friends as well as to be outside. God is Number One in her life.

Questions for Personal Reflection or Group Discussion

Mollie Astromowicz tells the story of an academic struggle that resulted in academic probation. This setback led to a period of deep personal reflection and a break from school, during which she reconnects with her faith and thinks deeply about her education and life goals.

Here are a few questions for personal reflection or group discussion:

1. Mollie faced a significant setback when put on academic probation. Reflect on a time when you faced a setback or failure. How did you respond, and what lessons did you learn?
2. Think about the benefits of taking time off during a stressful period to reassess goals. Have you ever taken a break that led to a new perspective or unexpected opportunities? Ponder the results that came with this decision.
3. Reflecting upon Romans 8:28, how do you reconcile personal challenges with the belief that everything happens for a reason?

14

THE PROMISE

BY DONNA BOLK

Prior to her heart operation, my mom was adamant that should anything go wrong, she didn't want to be put on machines. I was to be her voice. She left no doubt as to her final wishes. She said that if I didn't feel I could carry them out, she would find someone else. I promised her I would honor her requests.

A stroke during the operation left her unable to speak, and my mom lost the use of one side of her body.

Her mind was still sharp. She understood what was going on around her. It was painful to watch this once vibrant woman unable to do the simplest of things.

After several days, her doctor asked me to step into the hallway so we could discuss her medical condition and her options. I told him there was nothing wrong with my mother's mind; she could understand what he had to say, and she had the right to know her options.

The doctor wanted to hook her up to a machine and transport her to a nursing facility.

"Mom, do you understand what the doctor said?"

She nodded.

"Do you want to be hooked up to the machine and go to the nursing home?

She shook her head no.

"Mom, if you reject the machine, you will probably die."

She nodded again. Her eyes pleaded with me to keep the promise I had made to her.

I looked at the doctor. "You have her answer."

"Are you sure?"

"No," I whispered. "But she is." I smiled and squeezed her hand.

That night, they gave her a morphine drip to control the pain. My brother and I stayed by her bedside. I fell asleep holding her hand.

I woke late in the night to see her staring off in the distance. Her eyes were crystal clear, and she had the sweetest smile. I could tell she was seeing something or someone. I saw nothing, yet with all my being, I knew we were not alone.

I drew in a slow breath and held it, for in that blessed moment, I knew was witnessing a miracle. God was shining His light on my mom's path.

I'll never know who she saw that night. A family member? Her guardian angel? God?

I firmly believe that God has a plan for everyone. All things happen in His time.

The following day, my mom completed her heavenly journey. Two things I knew for sure: She wasn't alone, and I had done the right thing in honoring her last request.

To anyone facing what I did, I would say two things: It is never easy to say goodbye to a loved one, and promises made should be honored.

***

Prior to the release of her award-winning novel, *Saving Cinderella*, **Donna Bolk** wrote a column and human-interest features for the *Maryland Gazette*. She is a contributing author to *Words to Write By* (Mountain View Publishing). Prior novels from The Wild Rose Press include *Package Deal*, *Saving Cinderella*, and *Getting It Right*.

Questions for Personal Reflection or Group Discussion

Donna Bolk faced the profound responsibility of honoring her mother's end-of-life wishes after her mother suffers a debilitating stroke during hearty surgery. Respecting her mother's wishes, Donna declines the medical intervention. She experiences a powerful moment by her mother's side, perceiving a divine presence as her mother passes away peacefully.

Here are a few questions for personal reflection or group discussion:

1. Reflect on a time when you had to make or support a tough decision on behalf of someone else. How did you navigate the ethical or emotional challenges involved?
2. Ponder the importance of advocating for a loved one's wishes in medical settings. Why is it crucial to make sure their voice is heard?
3. Donna reflects on the idea that God has a plan for everyone, and that things happen in His time. How does this belief influence the way we cope with life's challenges and losses? Do you find comfort in this idea?

15

THE BALM OF GILEAD

BY LYNNE DRYSDALE PATTERSON

*B*efore you invited Jesus Christ into your heart, did you know that you live in a "fallen" world? Neither did I! Before I invited Jesus into my heart, the word *fallen* was simply the past tense of the verb *fall*. Yet, I suspected something was terribly "off."

Author J.R.R. Tolkien describes this sense of "off-ness" as an inkling, a vague understanding or notion. Picture a galvanized metal pail stuck on your head. Imagine trying to remove this pail, one inscribed with the words, "dead in your trespasses and sins" (Ephesians 2:1). Only after I invited Jesus into my life were the eyes of my heart opened. The pail was lifted! Jesus washed away my trespasses and sins with His precious, sinless blood. This was the dawn of my uncloudy day. I had entered the Kingdom of God. Sometimes referred to as "the land of milk and honey," my gospel ship docked on the pier of a new breed of people, too.

Recalling cherished memories of my grandmother's church from Sunday school days, I accepted an invitation to visit a beautiful church in Nashville with a carpeted choir loft and a married couple in charge of the music ministry. I had launched out into the unfamiliar deep of a new pond. Could this be what C.S. Lewis meant by his book titled *Mere Christianity*? A "mere" is defined as a pond or lagoon, specifically referring to a lake that is broad in relation to its depth. As a new fish in the pond, I quickly became disillusioned with in-house cliques who, in my opinion, did not reflect the love of God as I understood it.

After attending this church for several months, a married couple in the choir mentioned a church nearby and invited me to attend an evening service with them. I appreciated the pastor's message and was warmly welcomed by friendly parishioners. Several years later, I met my husband, Bruce, through mutual missionary friends attending this Holy Spirit-filled church.

Lifting my gaze from God's Word, I am ever mindful of newcomers to Christ, to His Church, and to those walking in darkness. I extend my hand and heart to them. We're commanded by Father God in His Bible to love our neighbor as ourselves ... and to be salt and light. Did you know salt heals wounds, and light helps replenish our cells and tissues?

When I see people, I recognize that Jesus died for each and every one. Encouraging people through God's Word can help heal hurts. In placing a poultice of love, peace, and joy—the spiritual balm of Gilead—on their wounded souls, I embrace the opportunity to *be* the gospel, a "do-er" of God's Word, not a hearer only.

* * *

Lynne Drysdale Patterson, award-winning songwriter, singer, and author, wrote *Taproots of Tennessee: Historic Sites and Timeless Recipes* (University of Tennessee Press) and *Taproots of Tennessee: The Companion Devotional*. Her middle grade stories are published by *Clubhouse Magazine*.

Questions for Personal Reflection or Group Discussion

Lynne Drysdale Patterson's story follows her transformative spiritual journey, starting from a place of not understanding the concept of a fallen world to experiencing a profound awakening upon accept Jesus Christ into her life. The story highlights Lynne's ongoing commitment to welcoming newcomers to Christ and the church, emphasizing that Christians are to be "salt and light" in the world—symbols of healing and rejuvenation.

Here are a few questions for personal reflection or group discussion:

1. Can you describe a moment when you felt like the "eyes of your heart" were opened? What was that experience like, and how did it change your life?
2. Have you ever felt disillusioned by a church or religious community? How did you navigate that disappointment, and what did you learn from the experience?
3. What does it mean to you to be "salt and light" in your community?

16

THERE IS HOPE IN JESUS

BY JACIE CONLEY

*I*t was the first Saturday in October, and the weather had cooled slightly. I had arrived at the doctor's building for my first mammogram. I was nervous because I had never been in this building, and I was unsure of the steps in getting a mammogram done.

I sat in the waiting room and people-watched. I took note of the doors and where they were taking people. I remember noticing one door and thinking, "I wonder where that door takes you?"

The staff were friendly, and I was in and out in less than thirty minutes. I was not worried about the results. I had no history of breast cancer in my family, and everyone had always received normal test results. I would be the first person where that changed.

The following Monday, I received an abnormal test result that showed two spots of concern. I had to report back for another mammogram and ultrasound.

I was concerned and shared the news with my family. I remember my church family gathering around me in a service and praying for God to intervene.

As I went for additional testing, I was hopeful. *God's going to take care of this,* I thought. The results of those tests were that I needed a biopsy.

Remember that door I noticed in the waiting room? I would now learn that is the door where they schedule patients for biopsies and oncology appointments. That's when I discovered that even though the test results may not be what you want, God is still with you. It wasn't exactly the news I wanted, but God gave me comfort and peace.

I broke down crying multiple times over the following month. I knew God would take care of me, but I was still human.

God exercised my faith during this time. A worship song would come on the radio, or we would sing one in church, and I would sob as I felt God's comforting presence and renewed hope. God, indeed, was my hope during this time.

At the end of October, I walked down a hallway toward a small room for my biopsy. The results turned out to be benign; those two spots were fluid-filled cysts that aspirated when biopsied. Praise God!

The one thought that kept running through my mind the entire time was, *How do people make it without hope from God?* When you face a similar trial or despair, remember that God offers hope. He is there in the hallways of uncertainty that we walk in life. God will be with you every single step of the way. He will never leave you. Walk through life knowing that there is hope and comfort in Jesus.

* * *

Jacie Conley is from Bristow, Oklahoma. She loves writing. Jacie has continued encouraging fellow Christians through her Daily Living Hope Facebook page. She prays that people struggling and needing hope find it through her writings.

Questions for Personal Reflection or Group Discussion

Jacie Conley tells about her emotional journey of undergoing her first mammogram, which unexpectedly shows abnormal results. She experiences deep anxiety and relies on her faith in God. The community's prayers and her own spiritual reflections sustain her as she faces further tests, including a biopsy that ultimately reveals the spots to be benign cysts.

Here are a few questions for personal reflection or group discussion:

1. Reflect on a time when you faced an unexpected challenge. How did it affect your emotional or spiritual life?
2. How do you express your emotions during times of uncertainty? What activities or practices provide you comfort?
3. Reflect on a time when you received good news after a period of worry. How did it change your perspective or approach to life's uncertainties?

17

A CHANCE TO FORGIVE

BY KELLI VASSO

"And when you stand praying, if you hold anything against anyone, forgive them, so that your Father in Heaven may forgive you your sins."
(Mark 11:25)

Was this my former teacher sitting in front of me? The man who humiliated, tortured, and embarrassed me? Who broke me down to have no value and defeated me? It took everything I had not to run.

The scene looked like every other day in my bank manager's office. As the man told me his plight, I asked God to help me remain kind.

How can he just sit there? Does he even know who I am? If he did, he wouldn't want my help. A stupid, dumb kid who couldn't read until thirteen, with debilitating dyslexia. God, do I help him?

I was a new Christian, and I knew God's grace and forgiveness. He forgave me with no condemnation. Yet I didn't want to extend grace to this man. He was my reason for fighting to do what others tell me I'm incapable of.

I decided to accept his loan application.

I went home that night and told my husband everything. We prayed and worshiped. I asked God to forgive me for harboring hate, to help me forgive my teacher.

The next morning, I went into work on a mission. I was going to bless this man who hurt me. I called the loan department, and they said no way. I called up the chain of command, called in all my favors, putting my reputation on the line.

I called, told the man I secured a loan, and set an appointment to sign the papers. I spent the next week praying, giving the situation to God. I didn't realize how much bitterness and hatred I still had inside me. I begged God to change my heart to see him as God sees him.

The day of the appointment, he was so thankful for a second chance. I sat and listened to his story about his daughters having health problems and learning disabilities. I was glad I chose God's way in this situation.

As he was ready to leave, I whispered, "You don't remember me, do you?"

He said, "Were you my student?"

"Yes, my name was Pirtel."

He cried. He said he thought about his unkindness toward me since he found out his own children had learning disabilities. He asked me how I could be so kind to him after all he had done to me.

I shared that I was a new believer in Jesus Christ. "God says I need to love my enemies, so I'm choosing to believe Him."

He apologized, and I accepted.

If you find yourself in a similar situation, trust God and choose kindness and forgiveness. Hopefully, it will lead them to a relationship with Jesus.

* * *

Kelli Vasso is a mom to five children and was a homeschooling mom. She is the owner of Kelli's Kitchen and The Hidden Place. The desire to write has been on Kelli's heart since her husband of thirty-five years passed away suddenly.

Questions for Personal Reflection or Group Discussion

In this story, Kelli Vasso encounters her former teacher who had previously demeaned and bullied her and now seeks her help with a loan. Despite her initial reluctance, she chooses to forgive and assist him, motivated by her newfound Christian faith and Scripture's teachings on grace and forgiveness. She goes to great lengths to secure the loan and receives an apology from the teacher. This story highlights themes of redemption and the power of forgiveness.

Here are a few questions for personal reflection or group discussion:

1. Kelli faced a profound, personal challenge when confronted with a former teacher who had been unkind to her. Reflect on a time when you had to decide between holding on to resentment or forgiving a person who hurt you. What factors helped influence your decision?
2. How can faith help us as we seek to overcome personal grievances?
3. How does understanding someone else's struggles influence your feelings toward them and your actions?

18

THE BLUES

BY SHARON KIRBY

I like the color blue; really, I do. It's the color of clear blue, sunny skies, and the gentle lapping waves of a quiet lake. But that day, I stared in unbelief at a blue spot that just happened to be on a white stick.

That's right. I was pregnant. Suddenly, unexpectedly, and inconveniently pregnant.

My husband and I had planned to wait until he had completed his master's degree before we started our family. But there we were, starting our family in spite of our plans.

You could call it failed birth control; we accepted it as God's timing, although we both panicked a bit during the first couple of weeks. How could we afford a baby? Could we manage on one income while he finished his degree? Where could we create a nursery in our small apartment? It didn't matter, for since this was clearly God's direction for our lives, He would work it out.

We traveled hundreds of miles to inform family and called others to announce our unexpected news. We were getting excited about our growing family.

One cold, December day, I stepped into the ladies' room, and my heart dropped. Soon my body showed ominous signs that everything was not well, and eventually we left the emergency room with a changed future.

I returned to work, pushing aside the blues that haunted me. A friend of mine who was also pregnant at that time took me aside to share her experience of surviving a miscarriage. She understood my pain and wrapped her arms around me physically and emotionally, starting the healing process from the loss of our little one.

Less than a month later, my friend once again miscarried, and the consoled became the consoler. I wondered if this was why I miscarried. Was it so that I could be her comforter, to be able to say I understood when no one else around her could?

Many years, another miscarriage, and two children later, I still don't have the answer to that query. I could presume that it was allowed so that I could better comfort others in their time of grief. Perhaps it was so that I learned to value every child's life through the lens of the miraculous. It could be a touch of Job—a time that was intended to shape and develop me.

In truth, I don't think I will ever know the exact "why" on this side of Heaven. What I do know for certain is that God uses everything—not just the happy things, but also the painful, the devastating, the unexpected—for our good when we are His (Romans 8:28).

And I can trust God with that.

* * *

Sharon Kirby lives in Michigan with her husband, Larry, and 007, their tuxedo cat. She is an award-winning author of short stories, author of the devotional *The Advent of Easter*, and a contributor to *Guideposts* magazine.

Questions for Personal Reflection or Group Discussion

When Sharon Kirby discovers she is pregnant, she feels overwhelmed and concerned about raising a child while her husband is still in graduate school. The couple gradually accepts and embraces the pregnancy as part of a divine plan. But their joy turns to sorrow when Sharon miscarries the baby, a loss that profoundly affects her. In her story, Sharon contemplates the possible reasons for her suffering and how it enables her to support others.

Here are a few questions for personal reflection or group discussion:

1. Reflect on a time when something unexpected shifted your plans. How did you adapt to the change?
2. How do you cope with loss and grief? What support systems are in place to help you during such times?
3. How does your faith in God help you to see the bigger picture, as described in Romans 8:28, during challenging times?

19

OUT OF THE DARKNESS

BY PAM WADDELL

*A*fter the movie, my date drove to a dark, secluded construction area. He had discovered my recent divorce and expected me to "pay" him for the movie. When I refused, he forced me into the back of his car and took what he wanted—driving me home afterward as if nothing happened. *Why?* my heart screamed, but I said nothing.

Shaken and trembling, I went inside. Grateful everyone was in bed, I took a hot shower to wash the filth off. Tears streamed down my face as I cried out to God. I decided not to tell my parents. They had helped me out of a short but abusive marriage and allowed me to start over. I'd caused them enough trouble.

Eventually, I got a job and settled into night classes, staying busy. I made a few friends at work. Life seemed normal. I prayed, but God seemed distant. I read my Bible, seeking answers, continually asking God for forgiveness for what happened that night. I attended worship services but got very little from them. I knew God was listening, if I could only hear Him.

A friend from work asked me to double date with her and a

friend of her boyfriend. I emphatically said, "No." She promised me it would be fun and I would be with her the whole time. I finally relented.

We went to the county fair. It was the first time I had enjoyed myself in a long time. I later learned Steve was not her boyfriend. She was only using him to make her boyfriend jealous.

A week later, Steve called and asked if I'd like to go hiking. Without hesitation, I said, "Sure!" We had a great time, talking all day. He asked if I'd like to go to church with him the next day, and I said, "Yes."

It was a small country church with his family and only a few more. I felt God's presence for the first time in a long time. Steve and I will celebrate our forty-ninth anniversary this August.

If you've endured a similar experience, don't give up. God hears your prayers. I couldn't hear Him, but He was listening. God answered my prayers.

Find someone you can confide in. That is one thing I wish I had done. Tell a trusted friend, pastor, or counselor. Trust in God to help you find your way out of the darkness and into His glorious light.

* * *

Pam Waddell is an award-winning author of short stories published by CWFL and *Guideposts* and co-author of *Simply His*, published by Alabama WMU. She has published articles in both *BSA* and *Contempo* magazines.

Questions for Personal Reflection or Group Discussion

The story recounts the harrowing experience of Pam Waddell who, after a recent divorce, is sexually assaulted by a date. The traumatic event leaves her feeling isolated and hesitant to burden her parents further, as they had previously helped her escape an abusive marriage. In the aftermath, she struggles with feelings of guilt and distance from God, despite her continued prayers and engagement with her faith in God. The story emphasizes the importance of seeking support, the healing power of companionship, and the resilience of faith through life's darkest moments.

Here are a few questions for personal reflection or group discussion:

1. How can one effectively process the trauma of sexual assault or abuse while maintaining or rebuilding faith?
2. Reflect on the importance of community and friendships in healing from personal trauma. How can these relationships provide support and help to rebuild trust?
3. How do you maintain your faith in God during periods when He seems distant or silent?

20

THE PROMISE OF A RAINBOW

BY MELISSA BROWN

*D*roplets dashed down my face faster than the rain on my windshield. The workday was filled with difficulty after difficulty, and my evening did not appear to be starting much better.

The long, thirty-minute route home was not helping my young daughter to calm down. Usually, a swaying vehicle was a mother's salvation, but apparently not even a car ride helped when little teeth were poking through your gums for the first time. After a challenging day at work, I was not sure I had the strength to endure the dual assaults of the piercing screams of my teething child and the pounding rain on my windshield.

To top it off, my ex-husband was being as accommodating as my uncooperative child. Being a single mother did not seem to be getting easier, but rather more challenging. And it was catching up with me on the highway.

The rain hit the glass harder, just like the water in my eyes, and my vision blurred. I pulled over and parked my gold Pontiac and allowed the tremendous tears to fall. I leaned my head on the steering wheel and sobbed.

God, I can't do this anymore, I cried out to God.

The cascading tears ran so quickly that my eyes dried out. My little girl's shrieks eventually turned to whimpers. I wiped my nose, took a deep breath, and lifted up my head. It was then that my saddened eyes turned into surprised eyes. I was in awe of what was in front of me.

Stretching widely over the entire area was a picturesque double rainbow. Hues of reds, oranges, yellows, blues, and even a row of violet permeated the afternoon sky. My heart began to soften as I was reminded of the promise God gave the world thousands of years ago. No matter how corrupt the world may become, He would never forsake us, and not ever flood the earth again.

This particular rainbow was so much more than that to me. This beautiful sight became an even deeper memento to me that God is ever so present in my current chaos. Just as He took the time to make this rainbow, He has taken the time to write the story of my little family. Though my present may feel uncertain, God has my future planned.

Although there are times when we will feel wrecked and wounded, we should do our best to pull over and "park" in our lives. When life gets too tough, and even unbearable, we can make it a practice to spend time crying out to God first. Seek Him in the car, the shower, the couch—wherever you are in your difficult moment.

His promise to be with you, wherever you may be, is guaranteed.

* * *

Melissa Brown has a passion for supporting and encouraging single mothers through her online platform, "Strong Single Momma." To receive encouragement and resources, check strongsinglemomma.com. Melissa lives with her daughter and pet birds, Skye and Mango.

Questions for Personal Reflection or Group Discussion

Melissa Brown, a single mother, shares one particularly challenging day as she drives home. Stressed by a hard day of work and her daughter's teething pain, she reaches a point of breakdown. She stops and cries for God's help. When she opens her eyes, she sees God's sign of His presence and reassurance in a beautiful double rainbow. The symbol of hope reminds her of God's divine plan for her and her daughter's lives.

Here are a few questions for personal reflection or group discussion:

1. Melissa experiences an overwhelming day that sends her into a moment of deep despair. She finds solace and assurance of God's presence in a double rainbow. Reflect on a time when you saw something that gave you much-needed comfort and hope.
2. Reflect on the idea of "parking" one's life to stop, reflect, and seek comfort. How important is it to take moments to pause and reflect during tough times?
3. How can expressing one's fears and frustrations to God help to cope with stress and hardship?

21

KEVIN'S STORY

BY ELLEN KOLMAN

How do I grieve the person I believed my child would grow up to be, but never will? This was the cold reality that slapped me in the face one afternoon in 1998.

My two-year-old son, Kevin, was diagnosed with autism in September 1995. By 1998, my husband and I were in the throes of rearing five young children while running five-year-old Kevin to every available therapy appointment, giving him the best interventions possible. We were hoping for a breakthrough, a cure, a chance for Kevin to experience life like everyone else.

On that afternoon, my son Alex innocently commented, "Mom, I don't think Kevin can get married."

"Why not?" I asked him.

"Because how will he ask her to marry him when all he can say is, 'doo-ee, doo-ee, doo-ee'?"

What should have been a cute anecdote was suddenly a vision of a different future I didn't want to see. But, at age five, Kevin was not saying words, and in every respect he was profoundly autistic and delayed. My heart was broken. We continued with the therapies and tried to find new ways to help

Kevin reach his optimal potential. But it was evident that Kevin's future was not going to be like other children's.

My internal conflict was palpable. I was grieving the son I thought he was going to be while feeling intense guilt because I was broken-hearted about his autism. Was my guilt valid? Did I not love my son just the way he was? After all, God created Kevin, and God does not make mistakes.

My husband said I was too hard on myself, that my grieving was natural, and he was grieving too. This declaration was a healing salve to my heart. My husband and I were in this together.

Time continued to fly by, and our children were growing up. Kevin did make some developmental strides forward, and everyone who worked with Kevin loved him. It was clear, however, that he would never be typical. Managing his own life, and potentially one day marrying, were not going to be for him, and that was okay.

It was okay. This realization didn't come in a bolt of lightning or from a bold vision from God. It came in the "still small voice," bit by bit, my heart healing a little more every day from just being Kevin's mom, praying for him, and loving him.

God's "grace is sufficient," and He has blessed Kevin with a plan and a purpose for his life. Now in his thirties, Kevin continues to teach all of us how to love others unconditionally and see every person as a precious gift from God.

* * *

Ellen Kolman is a wife, mother, grandmother, teacher, and author. Her published works include two children's books, *Sunshine Makes a Difference* (2024) and *Seeds of Sunshine* (2022) with Christian Faith Publishing. Visit her online at ellenkolman.com.

Questions for Personal Reflection or Group Discussion

Ellen Kolman tells her story of how she came to terms with her son Kevin's autism diagnosis. The story captures the internal conflict Ellen faces, dealing with her own sorrow while wrestling with guilt over feeling disappointed about Kevin's future. Over the years, Kevin makes some progress, and while it becomes clear he will not lead a typical life, the family learns to find joy and fulfillment in his unique journey. The story beautifully illustrates how the family's perspective evolves, recognizing that Kevin's life, though different, is not any less valuable.

Here are a few questions for personal reflection or group discussion:

1. How do you cope with the disparity between your hopes for your children and the reality of their abilities or choices?
2. What are some ways to find joy and fulfillment in raising a child who may not follow a typical developmental path?
3. How does faith in God help in coping with the challenges of raising a child with special needs?

22

TRUSTING IN THE DARK

BY JOYCE FARINELLA

"Would you take twin newborns who are coming into care?" my caseworker asked over the phone one afternoon.

"Yes!" My answer was immediate. I'd always wanted twins, but I didn't dream that I would get the chance as a single foster parent. I had only twenty-four hours to get ready.

The first few weeks were a whirlwind of activity with doctor's appointments and adjusting to schedules. The twins went to their mother's every weekend, which required me to meet her on Friday and Sunday afternoons. Though she came from a different world, I quicky developed a relationship with her. I wanted her to succeed, even though it would mean I would lose the twins.

I took the girls to church activities, county fairs, and a Fourth of July party as part of the family, along with my seven-year-old daughter. I watched my child jump into her role as big sister, playing with them, dressing them, and bathing them. She changed almost as many diapers as I did!

As the second court date loomed, the caseworker expected the judge to keep the same case plan. When he instead returned the girls to their mother, I swallowed the lump in my throat as I sat in shock, holding back the tears. Though I was happy for her, I was heartbroken for my family. She was gracious enough to give me the evening with the twins to say goodbye.

Still fighting off tears, I took the girls to their mother the next day. She promised to keep in touch, and I offered to babysit.

Darkness surrounded me for several days, reminders of the girls everywhere. I spent hours crying out to God, tears streaming down my face. Though I knew the decision was right for the twins and their mother, I still felt an acute sense of loss —a loss no one could understand unless they have been through a similar situation. I had lost my babies, children I had loved like my own, even though they weren't mine.

With a crushed spirit, I clung to the Bible verse that had been my lifeline throughout my fostering journey: Job 1:21b, "The Lord gave and the Lord has taken away; Blessed be the name of the Lord."

If you have suffered a similar loss, I would like to share a suggestion that helped me survive those dark days. I started praising God through my tears, thanking Him for the opportunity to have the babies for a few months. I learned that He was enough as He held me through my grief.

While God didn't take away my pain, He showed me that He was enough and walked with me through it.

* * *

Joyce Farinella is a full-time freelance content writer for businesses who is also beginning her career as a fiction writer with Christian cozy mysteries.

Questions for Personal Reflection or Group Discussion

As a single foster parent, Joyce Farinella is asked to care for twin newborns. She eagerly accepts, adjusting her life to accommodate the sudden responsibility. Over the following weeks, she forms a strong bond with the twins. The story peaks at a court decision to return the twins to their mother. The departure of the twins leaves Joyce with profound grief. She finds solace in her faith, particularly drawing strength from Job 1:21.

Here are a few questions for personal reflection or group discussion:

1. How can one prepare emotionally for the potential outcomes in foster care of similar situations where future uncertainties are significant?
2. In situations of loss, especially when losing someone close, how can individuals manage their grief in a healthy way?
3. What can the experience of caring for children teach us about love, loss, and resilience? Ponder a personal experience when this happened to you.

23

IT'S TOO MUCH!

BY SANDY ALSWORTH

I collapsed on the couch after a particularly brutal test. Three children. A job. Nursing school. What was I thinking? *God, please help me. It's too much!*

Knock, knock. My friends were at the door. Jobless. Homeless. Freezing. They wondered if the girls could stay overnight.

I ordered pizzas. My girls pulled their girls upstairs to play with the new dollhouse. *Thank you, Jesus, that I can help them.*

But the next day, there was another knock—a DHS worker. There were complaints. They were taking custody. Did we want to become foster parents?

No, Jesus, I can't! Not now. But wait. Where will these precious girls go? We've been friends for years. Jesus. What should I do? Well, okay. They can stay.

Why are crises so inconvenient?

Later, I curled up in a little ball and cried. *It's too much, God! I can't do this! Help me!*

His Spirit calmed me. I felt Him whisper, *What's important? Only do that. Nothing else. Take one day at a time. Trust Me.*

Okay, Jesus. Help me prioritize. I wrote a plan that included more fast food and less worrying about a clean house.

A few days later, my face was buried in a textbook. "Mom, can we go to the beach?" the kids interrupted with imploring eyes. "Please, Mom? Please?"

Well, I thought, *studying is a high priority, but so is making memories.*

"Okay, kids. Grab towels, water, and the dog. I'll grab my keys and textbook."

While they frolicked in the waves and buried each other in the sand, I sat on a piece of driftwood, shading the bright sun from my book with my hand. As I turned the pages, I wiped the sand off the book so it wouldn't leave little gritty bumps.

As my brain absorbed the knowledge that *borborygmus* refers to the sound of a hungry stomach, the fresh sea air and roaring waves were calming medicine for my soul.

Eight months later, the same week I started working as an RN, our friends' girls moved in with their grandparents. We cried. With God's help, it wasn't too much after all.

When life is too much for you to handle, tell Jesus. Let His loving Spirit calm you and teach you how to overcome. I needed to learn to prioritize, but He may have a different lesson for you.

"Let the morning bring me word of Your unfailing love, for I have put my trust in You.

Show me the way I should go, for to You, I entrust my life" (Psalm 32:8, NIV).

* * *

Sandy Alsworth is a wife, mother, and labor and delivery nurse on the Oregon coast. Her blog, SoundMindTalk.com, helps Christians find relief from anxiety and depression and includes the Bible, science, and personal experience.

Questions for Personal Reflection or Group Discussion

When Sandy Alsworth's friends need help, Sandy comes to their rescue, adding much more work and responsibilities to her heavy workload. But she receives God's reassurance to prioritize what's important and learns to manage one day at a time. This advice helps her balance her studies, personal life, and newfound foster responsibilities, focusing on what truly matters.

Here are a few questions for personal reflection or group discussion:

1. At what point do you recognize that your responsibilities are overwhelming you, and how do you respond?
2. How has faith in God played a role in making tough decisions in your life? Reflect on a time when this was particularly impactful.
3. How can small actions or moments, like a trip to the beach or a quiet minute alone, provide relief during stressful times? Think about a personal example from your own life.

24

THE GARMENT OF PRAISE

BY MARCEY STEVENS

Sometimes you just want to give up, and everything is a fight. You fight to get out of bed, take a shower, and do the things that most people do not give much thought to at all. Your mind seems to lock up either because thoughts have become scrambled or they disappear as if someone or something stole them away.

If you have never wrestled with a severe mental illness, this illustration may seem a bit dramatic. But if you have experienced this battle, you know exactly what I am talking about. In fact, you know it can be much worse than depicted here.

In 2006, I declared that I was happy, joyous, and free to a large crowd of people in a support group. During this experience, the Lord interrupted my own thoughts to say, *I won't let you fake it this time, Marcey.*

Wow, I thought. *That was loud and clear. Thank God that He has this way of grabbing my attention and redirecting me.*

Before receiving the keys to my freedom, I had wasted years fighting against this thing that was so much stronger than me. I eventually stopped trying to figure out which came first—the emotional break or the trauma. Now, my focus is Jehovah God who came running to my rescue despite myself and twenty-eight years of playing at church. I had been oblivious to the preciousness of God's grace; I was blind to His magnanimous mercy that had been playing like a beautiful symphony in the backdrop of my entire life.

I was stubborn, and I tried everything the world offers to fill the hole inside that left me miserable and even suicidal. But all attempts proved ineffective in matching an accurate depiction of the magnitude of His love for me.

The Lord Jesus has been relentless in His pursuit of my heart. I had to stop asking *why* or *how* He could, and instead be filled with great exuberance and pleasure that He chose me to be His. These things are too lofty and wonderful for me to comprehend and ascertain.

I can tell you, though, that no matter what you are facing in life, God's Word can be a powerful lifeline. I can also tell you that the shovel that will dig you out of the deepest, darkest, soul-sucking depression or paralyzing fear is gratitude.

If you wrestle with either of these, may I encourage you to redirect your focus to anything you can thank God for? Sing praises to the King of Glory. He invites us to take off the garment of heaviness and put on the garment of praise (Isaiah 61:3).

* * *

Evangelist **Marcey Stevens** has been delivered from addictions, obsessions, and gender identity confusion. She passionately pursues sharing with others the truth that set her free. Marcey enjoys life with her loving husband and their young grandson in Ohio.

Questions for Personal Reflection or Group Discussion

In this deeply personal story, Marcey Stevens shares her long-term battle with mental illness. She describes a pivotal moment in 2006, during a support group meeting, where a divine message awakened her and shifted her perspective from despair to hope. She finds solace and redirection in her faith.

Here are a few questions for personal reflection or group discussion:

1. Reflect on a personal challenge or condition that is hard for others to understand. How do you explain this to people who have not experienced it themselves?
2. Have you ever experienced a moment that felt like a direct intervention or message from God? How did it impact your decisions or beliefs?
3. Share how practicing gratitude has affected your life. Can you think of a specific instance where being grateful changed your perspective or situation? If so, please reflect on the lessons you learned.

25

HEALING FROM WORKPLACE TRAUMA

BY B. ANNE STEVENS

"If you tell anyone about this meeting, I'll lie about it, and so will you," my boss hissed from across the table. After everything I'd done for this job, telling me to lie was the last straw. I calmly walked out of the office that day in June 2015.

While sobbing in the car, my trembling fingers dialed the number for an employment attorney. My subsequent formal complaint ended a two-year-long work environment that included sexual harassment, bullying, and emotional abuse. The days that followed turned into tumultuous months of legal processes. The day his resignation was announced, female co-workers came to thank me.

I recovered, but healing from the workplace abuse was easier than dealing with lingering guilt. As a Christian, I tried to be a godly example of integrity in the workplace, yet I had allowed a toxic emotional attachment to cloud my judgement. How did I get entangled in such an unhealthy professional relationship for two years? There were valid reasons, but not all reasons were good excuses. I ignored red flags because I was successful at my job. The good outweighed the bad because I thought I was making a difference. Confusion skewed my thinking, as often happens in abuse. Part of me let it happen.

Abuse is *sin*—fueled by deception, manipulation, and control. One day it hit me that I participated in the sin by keeping silent. I allowed inappropriate behavior to keep the peace. Sometimes I even complied with wrongful directives that hurt others. I was an *accessory*.

"It's not your fault," others said. "You're a victim. He abused his power." I understood all that, but I could have done many things differently.

A year later, in a park surrounded by the colors of fall, I thanked God for helping me through the whole ordeal. Yet, I still felt guilty. As I begged God for forgiveness, a still small voice cut through the crisp air.

"I have pardoned you."

Pardoned. That word hung clear as I considered what it meant. God not only forgave me, but He understood what happened, and He didn't hold it against me. He didn't hold me responsible. The slate was wiped clean. Pardoned. The guilt was gone!

If you are dealing with how to heal from a similar workplace experience, something that brought me wholeness was a two-part approach: 1) forgiving the individual who harmed me, and 2) forgiving myself for my part in it, even though it may have been out of my control. God understands your situation. He has a way out and a way forward. You can't mess up His plan for your life!

* * *

B. Anne Stevens writes inspiring true stories to share God's love. She enjoys life in the St. Louis area with her husband, six sons, and two grandsons. You can find her online at www.bannestevens.com.

Questions for Personal Reflection or Group Discussion

B. Anne Stevens's story captures her journey through a toxic work environment that escalated to sexual harassment, bullying, and emotional abuse. After enduring this for two years, she resigns and seeks legal recourse. Through a process of self-reflection and spiritual guidance, she reaches a point of forgiveness—both for herself and her abuser, healing her and giving her a hopeful future.

Here are a few questions for personal reflection or group discussion:

1. How can individuals navigate feelings of guilt or complicity in situations where they were manipulated or coerced? Ponder the balance between personal responsibility and victimization.
2. How can spiritual beliefs and practices and faith in God aid in recovering from emotional and psychological wounds inflicted in professional settings?
3. What steps can be taken to prevent harassment and abuse in the workplace? What are some signs of a toxic work environment, and how can one address them without compromising personal integrity or professional responsibilities?

26

KNOCKED DOWN, BUT NOT KNOCKED OUT

BY MEL TAVARES

"You need a total knee replacement." These were not the words I wanted to hear from the orthopedic surgeon. Plead as I might, he reiterated that surgery was my only option to repair the extensive damage done during the accident. "Your recovery time will be six to twelve months." Numb, I left and drove to the coffee shop to drown my sorrows in my favorite latte.

As I sipped, I reflected on this latest life punch in the list of traumatic events that had started two months prior on Labor Day weekend. I'd been looking forward to a long weekend and was unprepared to hear, "You've done nothing wrong; we are just going in a different direction." With those words, my job was eliminated, effectively immediately. I cleaned out my desk and left the building, feeling rejected and unwanted.

In the morning, faith arose in my spirit. Ignoring my jobless reality, I found my gardening gloves and decided to help my husband trim our hedges.

My husband's voice broke through my thoughts. "Run!" My attempt to outrun the swarm of yellow jackets surfacing from the nest hidden in the hedges was in vain. I tripped and heard a thud, barely registering the fact that I was lying in the street being stung repeatedly while my mangled knee refused to allow me movement.

Sitting at the urgent care facility, tears streamed down my face. I'd allowed onlookers to believe they were from knee pain, but the truth is the weekend events had rendered me unable to get up off the proverbial mat. My grieving spirit was crushed.

Despite trying to understand God's ways, I couldn't comprehend how life coming to a screeching halt made sense when ministry momentum had been building for the past year. I had struggled for months to regain my physical and mental health, and now the surgeon had just informed me of the need for a total knee replacement. I knew surgery would mean more pain, more of a financial drain, and another delay in my ability to work. It felt like the knock-out round, just for a moment.

If you find yourself wounded and lying on the mat of life, may I share a suggestion that helped me? I had to accept that unexpected things happen to all of us, and we are typically not in control of changes we suddenly find ourselves facing. I had to decide to trust God and His promises for my future and purposefully rise up off the mat.

Savoring the last sip of the latte, I prayed for strength to move forward, knowing I was knocked down but not knocked out..

* * *

Dr. Mel Tavares is an award-winning, multi-genre author. Her best-selling book, *21 Days to Improved Mental Well-Being*, is a helpful tool for those needing to rise up. Learn more at drmeltavares.com.

Questions for Personal Reflection or Group Discussion

Mel Tavares experienced an unexpected job loss during a holiday weekend, as well as a frightening accident involving a swarm of yellow jackets that resulted in a severely damaged knee. She underwent a total knee replacement and faced a lengthy recovery period, making her feel overwhelmed by the physical, emotional, and financial toll of these setbacks. In a moment of deep reflection at a coffee shop, Mel finds a moment of clarity and prays for the strength to move forward, embracing the idea that although knocked down, she was not knocked out.

Here are a few questions for personal reflection or group discussion:

1. How do you cope with sudden, unexpected life changes?
2. How does your faith in God influence your recovery from personal setbacks or health issues?
3. Reflect on a time when you felt emotionally overwhelmed by multiple challenges. What steps did you take to regain your composure and strength?

27

FORGIVENESS AND OPPORTUNITY

BY SUSAN KING

*I*f there was ever a phrase that could have been tattooed on my forehead, it was, *Don't question my work ethic!* If a side-eyed glance was given by a co-worker questioning my moral conduct, internally, I would explode.

But at some point, as with all buried misdeeds, the rain fell hard enough to reveal the sin beneath the soil. The sunlight hit it for all to see, and when revealed, there were two choices to make. I could stomp it into the ground, hoping no one would notice; or, I could drop to my knees in the garden and ask forgiveness of God, take the weed whacker of God's Word and pulverize it, and ask for guidance to not fertilize that growth of thorns ever again.

Having left my last job before I could be terminated, I had been applying for new positions. Being gifted by God with talents to serve others, I had been blessed to work within the nonprofit industry for over twenty years. In that time, God had given me skills that some of my co-workers had to invest time and money in for their degrees in social work. But I was a high school dropout with a GED. After many years of challenging work, a supervisor promoted me into a position that should have only been held by a college graduate.

Somewhere along the way, I lost my gratitude. My mouth would still praise God for the financial security I had and the patience He would pour into me in as I dealt with challenging clients, but my heart had turned dark toward my leadership. My only prayer concerning them was for God to remove them. But God allowed a bad decision I had made to be revealed, and He moved me instead.

My search for a new position was challenging as paranoia set in. *Lord, please give me favor with my interviewer in the position you want me to have,* I prayed. I awoke the morning of yet another interview expecting to be rejected again.

Within that forty-five-minute meeting, I experienced the like-mindedness of a godly man who has been a pastor for twenty-five years, and who could not even complete the interview without telling me how excited he was that I had applied. I had not even made it home before he called and officially offered me the job.

At this writing, I feel this new manager will be a mentor and help smooth out the edges of my negative characteristics in the workplace that were dishonoring to God. Being humbled is not a pleasant experience, but I have an anticipatory joy about my future, knowing it will be necessary for growing deeper in obedience to God.

* * *

Susan King is a published author who embraces her gift of transparency, believing the honest sharing of the human experience, coupled with relationship with God, can impart healing to others.

Questions for Personal Reflection or Group Discussion

In this story, Susan King tells about a time when she stopped and reflected on her past attitudes and actions and recognized a lack of connection between her professed faith and her actions. She confronted a struggle, learning from it and asking God for forgiveness and guidance.

Here are a few questions for personal reflection or group discussion:

1. Reflect on a time when you had to confront your own flaws or mistakes openly. What did you learn from that experience?
2. Susan's story deals with the tension between outward expressions of faith and internal spiritual struggles. How do you make sure your external actions reflect your true inner beliefs, values, and spiritual faith?
3. How important is mentorship or guidance in your life, and who has been a mentor to you? In what ways have they helped you?

28

THE NURSE IN BLUE SCRUBS

BY TAMMY MOSER

I sat in the driver's seat, gripping the steering wheel and waiting for my friend to get off work. I was on vacation for a week and visiting her from North Carolina. She had a wonderful position at Cedars-Sinai hospital in Los Angeles, a prestigious career making good money.

I, on the other hand, was barely scraping by in a job that was leading me nowhere. I desperately wanted to do something more meaningful but felt completely hopeless.

As I stared through the windshield in a daze, my eyes became fixed on a nurse in blue scrubs walking through the parking lot. I imagined she was on her way to start the evening shift. My heart sank as I began to think, *If only I could be someone like that.* I couldn't imagine having the ability or confidence to become a nurse.

Honestly, I had never even entertained the thought until that moment. It seemed like such a noble profession, but one completely unattainable for me. You see, I had given my heart to the Lord as a young child, but bad choices in high school and college had taken their toll on my spiritual walk. The heaviness of life without Jesus clouded my decisions and felt like a thick fog enveloping my path. I couldn't figure out the way ahead. I had graduated with a degree in interior design, but my confidence was at an all-time low, and I never pursued work in that field.

Looking back on that day, however, it is evident the Lord had graciously given me a vision of what was to come. Several years after that visit, I started taking science classes to apply for physical therapy school, but I was rejected.

However, God's plans always prevail, because eventually, I was accepted into a bachelor's program for nursing. It was there, while in school, alone in my apartment one night and tired of carrying life's heavy burdens, that I pulled out a Bible to read.

As I prayed, tears streamed down my cheeks and my eyes fell to the words "Cry unto me and I will rescue you and you will give me glory" (Psalm 50:15, NIV). I knew in that instant, like the prodigal child coming home, that His arms were wide open to receive me.

I have been a nurse for the past thirty-four years and wearing blue scrubs for twenty-four. It has been an amazing adventure with the Lord!

Does your life feel hopeless and without purpose? Jesus stands at the door of our hearts and knocks. He longs to be gracious to you. Will you choose to let Him in?

* * *

Tammy Moser grew up in Bellemont, North Carolina, next to her grandparents. In addition to her nursing career, she began writing five years ago and published a book in 2022, *Divine Encounters on a Cancer Floor.*

Questions for Personal Reflection or Group Discussion

Tammy Moser grappled with feelings of inadequacy and lack of direction while comparing herself to a successful friend. A visit to Los Angeles sparked the thought of pursuing a nursing career, despite feeling utterly unqualified and disconnected from her faith. This moment of introspection marked a turning point in Tammy's life. Her story highlights the unpredictable nature of life's journey, the power of vocational calling, and the grace of rediscovering faith.

Here are a few questions for personal reflection or group discussion:

1. Reflect on a time when you experienced a turning point in your career or personal life. What sparked the change, and how did it shape your path forward?
2. How do you deal with feelings of inadequacy or comparisons to others' successes?
3. How has your faith in God influenced your career choices or helped you through professional and personal challenges?

29

CHANGE REQUIRED

BY PHIL BRAY

My cousin slumped at the kitchen counter, head in his hands. His nights as a shift worker had come to an unexpected crashing halt.

The next morning, there I was, sitting on a plastic stackable chair, sandwiched between a photocopier and a pile of Bible study booklets, sharing the distressing story.

"He's been struggling for a long time, and shift work hasn't helped his feeling of isolation. He's been trying to come to church more regularly since his girls started youth group, but losing his job has broken him." I then had the audacity to ask if someone from the pastoral care team might reach out and give him a phone call.

My minister's mouth curled into an attempted smile that more resembled a sneer. "Well, the way we do pastoral care at our church is in Bible study groups, and I have spoken to him several times about joining one, but I suppose he's never made it a priority. Our door is always open, though, if he ever wants to come back to church."

I left that meeting fighting back tears, fists clenched so tight that my fingernails drew blood.

That week I hardly slept, ruminating on all the things I should have said to highlight the minister's hypocrisy. *You're a minister yet you lack mercy. You're supposed to be a shepherd yet you've abandoned your sheep.*

As the conversation replayed in my mind, the ammunition that brought the most decisive victory was the biblical story of the woman at the well. Jesus wasn't hiding inside a building, requiring her to join a Bible study. He reached out and He spoke to her—*first*. She was woman who didn't go to the right church; she was the kind of person Jesus should not have been speaking to. Yet He had compassion for her, and He loved her.

A recent night began the same way as most other nights, but it ended by highlighting my need for repentance. My son had been waiting all week to kick some goals with me. I arrived home as usual, and as usual, I noticed the mess.

"Who left honey on the bench?" I asked. "Do those shoes belong on the kitchen floor? Have you done your homework? Let me know when you've finished your chores and then maybe we can hang out."

My son stormed past me, fists clenched, blinking back tears. Then I noticed his soccer ball.

My dear reader, if you love your kids, your partner, your parents, remember Jesus at the well, smiling with compassion at a woman He'd never met before. Reach out and love them—first —before imposing any requirements. I took the first steps of a lifelong commitment that night:

I picked up the ball and went to find my son.

* * *

Phil Bray lives in Sydney Australia. His favorite book is Leviticus, and when he's not fixing coffee machines, he's writing about ancient sacrifice, atonement, and scapegoats. You can read his stuff at ubiquitousleviticus.com.

Questions for Personal Reflection or Group Discussion

The story revolves around Phil Bray's concern for his cousin, a shift worker who has recently lost his job, compounding his existing struggles with isolation and a desire to connect with his church community. Phil then draws a profound connection to his own near-missed opportunity to connect with his son over soccer. When Phil puts aside his distractions and expectations, he's able to show love to his son in the same way Jesus showed love toward the woman at the well in John 4.

Here are a few questions for personal reflection or group discussion:

1. How important is it for community leaders, like pastors or ministers, to provide personalized support? Ponder an experience where you felt supported or unsupported by your community.
2. What are some barriers people might face when trying to engage more with their church or community group? How can these groups include more diversity of people?
3. Reflect on a time when you realized you needed to practice more compassion in your personal relationships. What prompted this realization, and how did you respond?

30

WALKING BY FAITH

BY JANE REESE

"For we walk by faith, not by sight." We have heard this passage in 2 Corinthians 5:7 many times. For me, it became literal.

I was struggling to break free of alcoholism, reeling in the ashes of mistakes I made. I entered a recovery program that involved working in a country cafe four days a week. Three months in, I slipped in the cafe kitchen, fell on the concrete floor, and fractured my lumbar spine. Within two days, walking on my right leg became excruciating.

I had to leave the recovery program and return to my best friend's couch to live, using a wheelchair to get around. I had no health insurance but was able to have an MRI that revealed a compressed sciatic nerve causing the pain and loss of function in my right leg. There was no way for me to pay for the care I needed to repair the damage. I was without hope.

I began attending a small church where I met a group of amazing people who inspired me with their faith and love for Jesus. They accepted me in all my brokenness and encouraged me to read Scripture, pray, and seek God's will for my life. They prayed over me at the altar each week, and one Sunday, I stood up. The following week, God spoke to me and told me to put away the wheelchair, and I did.

There is no explanation for my healing other than my Lord and Savior. Finally, I was listening closely enough to hear His voice. My prayers, pleas, and persistence took me, at last, to a place where my faith conquered my fear. I kept walking. Daily, I get up from my bed and say a quiet word of gratitude to the Lord for my legs.

Friend, if you are in a dark place, start looking up. In Jeremiah 29:13, the Lord says, "If you seek me wholeheartedly, you will find me." Pray, read, and believe. Know that an answer will come, and pray for God's help to accept His answer and move forward.

Walking by faith means being absolutely convinced that God is listening. God used my fractured spine to lead me to the place where I could find peace, knowing that I would be alright whether walking or in a wheelchair. Praise God that I continue to walk by faith. My physical injury led me to my spiritual healing, and in my journey, I learned that my spiritual walk is infinitely more important than being able to stand on two legs as I walk through this life.

* * *

Jane Reese, sixty-three, is a retired RN and aspiring Christian writer. She lives in San Antonio, Texas, with her beloved ginger tabby cat, Leo. She is proud to have had two essays chosen for publication previously by Christian Writers for Life.

Questions for Personal Reflection or Group Discussion

Jane Reese, struggling with alcoholism and the life disruptions it caused, finds a glimmer of hope in a recovery program. However, an unfortunate accident at work leads to a severe spinal injury and further complicates her path to recovery. Jane turns to a small church community where the warmth and support of its members inspire a deep spiritual awakening in Jane. Through persistent prayer and divine intervention, Jan realizes a profound spiritual renewal.

Here are a few questions for personal reflection or group discussion:

1. How can the support of a church and community play a role in one's recovery from unexpected crises?
2. How does a deep faith in God and His Word influence healing and recovery in the face of physical and emotional challenges?
3. How can God's Word provide comfort and guidance during tough and painful times?

31

CINNAMON AND APPLES NO MORE

BY SARA THORNBURGH

Growing up, for most of our fall family meals, specifically for fall holidays, we'd gather for lunch or dinner around a table decorated in autumn themes and colors.

This meal always consisted of turkey or ham, green bean casserole, and all the other "usuals" such as rolls, yams or sweet potatoes, cranberry sauce, pickles, olives (that children and even adults playfully put on their fingers), and, of course, mouthwatering desserts like pumpkin pie, apple pie, lemon meringue pie, cinnamon rolls, and more.

During these meals, we were always reminded to be thankful for what we'd been given, and why it's important to be grateful and thankful. These are memories I'll never forget and will always cherish.

Over the years, I grew to like most of the foods I didn't care for when I was younger, but soon an unexpected wrench would be thrown into my family celebrations.

I found out a couple of years ago that I am allergic to apples and cinnamon. Thankfully I'm not deathly allergic, but I'm allergic enough to cinnamon that I can't be around it at all or I will have a severe coughing attack until the cinnamon or cinnamon fragrance is removed. My allergy to apples isn't quite as severe, unless they're combined with cinnamon.

Having these allergies has definitely helped me be more compassionate than I already was toward those who have it worse than I do, because now I can truly relate to what they go through.

I don't know what it's like to have food allergies as a child, or to have them my entire life. But I can definitely tell you from my experience that being able to eat things like pumpkin pie and apple pie for your entire life, and then having them suddenly taken away from you, is not fun or easy.

Fall and winter are the hardest for me since during those times of year, food and drinks with these ingredients abound, along with their fragrances.

These new allergies have been a good reminder to me that it is possible to become allergic to anything at any time, no matter how old you are. I'm reminded not to take anything for granted.

I'm praying, hoping, and believing that the Lord will heal me and every other person who suffers from food allergies.

However, until He does, I continue to learn how to navigate having food allergies as an adult. But I do believe He is Jehovah-Rapha, our God who heals, because He has healed me in the past.

And He can heal you too.

* * *

Sara Thornburgh is an emerging writer and author with three award-winning stories: "Cherished Memories," "Make a Joyful Noise," and "Fall Foods." You can find out more about Sara's work at "Sara Thornburgh—Author" on Facebook.

Questions for Personal Reflection or Group Discussion

In this story, Sara Thornburgh reflects on cherished memories of family gathering during fall holidays, highlighting the warmth and joy of shared meals adorned with festive decorations and traditional dishes. The story takes a twist when Sara discovers she has developed allergies to apples and cinnamon as an adult. This new challenge brings a deeper empathy for others with similar or worse conditions, and it prompts a reflection on the unpredictable nature of life and health.

Here are a few questions for personal reflection or group discussion:

1. How have your traditions or abilities to participate in them changed over time? How do you maintain a sense of gratitude despite these changes?
2. How has a personal challenge or health issue helped you develop empathy and understanding for others?
3. How does your faith in God influence your response to personal health challenges? Ponder how your spiritual beliefs have provided support or solace during difficult times.

32

LOVE TAKES NO ACCOUNT OF THE WRONG DONE TO IT

BY REBECCA A. OWENS

For Christmas, I gifted a family member a book in which one of my short stories was published. Neatly wrapped, with a bow on top, I waited excitedly as the present was opened.

"What is this?" Holding the book in their hand, forehead wrinkled, they looked at the book with a confused expression.

"It's an anthology, with Christian short stories," I smiled. "All the stories are written with the same theme. Flip to the bookmark." I pointed to the extra gift included in the book. "That's my short story."

"Oh." Setting the book on the side table, they turned to the teenage girl sitting beside them. "You're a senior this year—are you excited? Have you started shopping for prom dresses?"

My shoulders slumped, and I looked from one person to the next in confusion and disbelief. No one said anything, not even "congratulations."

Tears filled my eyes, and I turned to stare at the beautifully decorated Christmas tree. I had danced with excitement when I received the news that my short story had been selected to be published. Seeing my name and my story in print uplifted my spirit and gave me confidence that my stories mattered.

In one evening, all my confidence and joy in writing was destroyed by those closest to me.

How could my family dismiss me? It didn't take long for my disappointment to turn into anger. I pushed to my feet and escaped to the kitchen to wash the dinner dishes. The conservations in the other room continued, and my eyes burned and watered while I cleaned and waited for the right time to leave and go home.

As I put the leftovers from dinner into the refrigerator, a photo on the wall caught my attention. There were nine hearts, each decorated differently with flowers and ribbon with pink, baby blue, green, and white daisies. Each heart had writing beginning with the word "Love.

Love is patient, love is kind. Love does not envy, love does not boast, and love is not proud. Love is not rude, love always trusts, love always hopes, and love never fails.

Love takes no account to the wrong done to it.

I let the words sink in. It wasn't right for me to have hard feelings; it was Christmas after all. No matter how much my family hurt me, I love them and I needed to forgive them. I bowed my head and prayed.

The moment I forgave my family, the disappointment and hurt vanished. I made a pot of coffee and helped serve dessert.

When our hearts have been hurt, we should remember that Jesus first loved us, and in order to love Him, we have to forgive.

* * *

Rebecca A Owens writes wholesome romance and Christian devotions and is a Native American sensitivity reader. She is currently working on a Christian memoir, *Anchored by Hope*. Rebecca can be reached on her website, rebeccaaowens.com.

Questions for Personal Reflection or Group Discussion

Rebecca A. Owens highlights a personal experience when, during a family Christmas gathering, she presents a family member with a book that includes one of her published short stories. Rebecca's anticipation turns to disappointment when her gift and accomplishment are met with indifference, leading to a profound sense of rejection and a questioning of her worth and talent as a writer. But after a moment of reflection, prompted by a display about love from 1 Corinthians 13, she forgives them, recognizing that love involves overlooking wrongs. She realizes that her value as a writer didn't diminish because of others' lack of recognition.

Here are a few questions for personal reflection or group discussion:

1. Reflect on a time when you felt overlooked, and how you coped with that feeling.
2. What are some healthy ways you've found to deal with disappointment, especially when it comes from those we love?
3. How can one maintain self-esteem and confidence when faced with rejection or indifference from others?

33

LIQUID SUNSHINE

BY CAROL V. MEYER

*S*tubborn sobs rattled my frame as melodic voices cradled my heart before colliding with brokenness. I gulped—a futile effort to temper the torrent of grief my fellow day-retreaters' anthem unleashed. They were singing "Amazing Grace," and I was unable to sing. Singing was one of my great loves, and "Amazing Grace" a favorite hymn.

I entered this wilderness at the beginning of 2020 when Recurrent-Voice-Loss befriended Chronic-Fatigue. This destructive alliance dismantled the potential of my conducting occasional workshops or accepting speaking invitations again. I sought solace in Scripture, listened to worship music, created art, and wrote extensively. These nourishing practices were like liquid sunshine in my unconventional cocoon.

By mid-2023, episodes of continuous voicelessness spanned months. Hope's candle began to splutter, and the notion of recovery waned like a withering vine. Hollow eyes surveyed the desolate Valley of Broken Dreams. It wasn't long before Madam Self-Pity arrived; she was decked out in her finest as she galloped onto center stage. Then, I descended into Discouragement's nearby lair.

Several new moons later, I came to myself. *God is always with me. When I feel isolated behind thick walls of fatigue, brain-fog, silence, or a hoarse croak, He hears the cry of my heart. God will fulfil His plans for me, whatever that looks like in this season. I may not know what my future holds, but I know Who holds my future.* With renewed hope, I gave Madam the boot, left the lair, and once more, liquid sunshine prevailed.

As I persevere and navigate this winding road, I cherish God's Word. I particularly love revisiting the Gospels. Scripture also helps to silence rogue thoughts and generate hope. *My Heavenly Father cares for me; He loves and helps me—He is more than enough.*

Although debilitating fatigue and voice challenges persist, I've learned to be content. While I can't currently accept invitations that involve speaking, who knows what tomorrow may bring? So, in one of my hands, I hold acceptance of "what is," and in the other, extravagant hope.

If you're facing discouragement, may I suggest two practices that help me? One: find and meditate on Scriptures that encourage. Two: reflect on what God's already done for you; write it down or record it electronically, so you can read it again and again. I love reading my "thank you journal," an electronic document I started in 2016. When I reflect on God's faithfulness and goodness to me in the past, it stirs deep thankfulness. Then, when I consider that my God is omnipotent, omnipresent, omniscient, and unchanging, this strengthens my faith and brings sunshine to rainy days.

* * *

Carol V. Meyer is a writer, poet, and artist. She feels blessed that three of her stories have been published in two CWFL anthologies.

Questions for Personal Reflection or Group Discussion

In this deeply personal narrative, Carol V. Meyer explores her journey through a debilitating period marked by voice loss and chronic fatigue. These conditions prevented her from participating in cherished activities like conducting workshops and singing. She turns to her faith in God for solace and strength, reaffirming her faith in God's presence and plan, regardless of her physical limitations.

Here are a few questions for personal reflection or group discussion:

1. How do you manage the emotional and psychological impact of chronic health conditions?
2. How has your faith in God influenced your response to personal challenges? Reflect on a time when this was particularly significant.
3. How do you find the balance between accepting your current circumstances and maintaining hope for the future? Think back on personal experiences where this balance proved crucial.

34

CONFRONTING CANCER WITH HOPE

BY LANA WYNN SCROGGINS

*S*tanding beneath the sprawling branches of the towering oak tree, I felt the weight of the world crashing down upon me. What began as a routine checkup, a mere formality to fulfill insurance requirements, spiraled into something infinitely more profound.

It had been ages since I last graced the doors of a doctor's office; after all, I was seldom plagued by illness. Little did I know that this visit would alter the course of my life in ways I could never have imagined.

Sent across the street to a hospital for what I assumed were mundane tests, I encountered a technician who defied convention. Technicians, as a rule, refrained from divulging test results to patients. But she felt compelled to show me.

With trembling hands, she pointed out the ominous shadows on the screen—shadows that whispered of an insidious intruder: cancer. Disbelief coursed through me like a tidal wave, yet seeds of doubt took root in the recesses of my mind.

Walking into the doctor's office, I braced myself for the inevitable. The doctor was kind as he gave me the results. As his words washed over me, I found myself adrift in a sea of despair.

Breast cancer. The diagnosis hung in the air, heavy with implications. I had arrived at this appointment alone, oblivious to the tempest that awaited me. Reality blurred, and I struggled to grasp the enormity of what lay ahead.

Amidst the chaos, a beacon of light emerged in the form of an angelic nurse. With compassion etched into every line of her face, she extended a lifeline to a drowning soul.

"I have nursing friends, ready to guide you through every step," she assured me, as she handed over a meticulously organized plan of action. Gratitude swelled within me, a flicker of hope amidst the encroaching darkness.

Seeking solace, I sought refuge beneath the sprawling branches of the oak tree. There, amidst the whispering leaves, I offered up a simple prayer to God that I needed help in the face of overwhelming adversity.

Summoning the courage to confide in a friend, I shattered the suffocating silence that threatened to consume me. She assured me that together, we would navigate the treacherous waters of uncertainty, fortified by our unwavering faith in God.

The journey ahead loomed dauntingly, fraught with uncertainty and fear. Yet, in the depths of despair, I found a glimmer of hope. As I wrestled with the tumultuous emotions swirling within, I held to the unwavering belief that I am not alone. With each passing day, I drew strength from God and His love that surrounded me, steadfast in my resolve to weather the storm with resilience and grace.

* * *

Dr. Lana Wynn Scroggins, a writer and speaker, shares Jesus through her Giving Jesus website offering devotionals, activity books, and the gift guide *Ink & Faith Reads* for faith-based authors in which she curates diverse books for gift-giving opportunities. Lana, based in a coastal community, centers her days on faith, her business, and writing.

Questions for Personal Reflection or Group Discussion

A routine medical checkup uncovers a diagnosis of breast cancer, sending Lana Wynn Scroggins into a spiral of shock and despair. In the midst of the turmoil, a compassionate nurse offers Lana a structured plan and support, lighting a path forward. This act of kindness injects a sliver of hope into Lana, prompting her to seek solace and strength in the company of a supportive friend. Together, they resolve to face the upcoming challenges with faith and courage.

Here are a few questions for personal reflection or group discussion:

1. Reflect on the impact that compassionate care from medical professionals can have during a health crisis. Have you experienced a situation where a medical professional went beyond a clinical role to offer support?
2. Ponder the role of friends and community in navigating personal crises. How important is it to have a support network?
3. What are some ways to cultivate and maintain hope when facing a daunting journey like a serious illness?

35

SURVIVOR

BY ROSE WALKER

I'd had a fibrocystic condition on my left side for years and hypochondria my whole life. I didn't bother with self-exams. My gynecologist said to notice if something was different. The summer before my fortieth birthday, that *something* was a hard knot on my right breast. Still afraid of looking stupid for overreacting, I waited until I actually turned forty to have that recommended first mammogram.

"Probably nothing to worry about," my gynecologist said, "but let's get your scan set up."

I thought, "Um, it's probably *something* …"

I had to go to a nearby town because the local machine wasn't working. Before that Monday appointment, I lay down for my typical Sunday afternoon nap. Unsure if it was a dream or an auditory vision, I clearly heard a familiar male voice (maybe my long-deceased father's—his first wife had died of breast cancer) say, *Rose has cancer in her right breast.* The nurse called Monday afternoon telling me that calcifications showed up there, and I would need a biopsy.

In my recovery room, the surgical nurse cried, knowing I

had three young children. In a whirlwind over the next few weeks, we consulted with doctors and lined up a mastectomy with partial reconstruction, chemo, and radiation. My surgery was in early December 2000, and treatment covered most of the next year.

At diagnosis, believing I'd received a death notice, depression set in. I began planning a funeral and worried about leaving my beautiful babies without a mama.

But the surgeon who'd done the biopsy said, "Oh no, you need to be planning what flowers and music to have at your daughters' weddings!"

I soon began meeting and learning of survivors—one year, five years, ten, twenty, forty—living life and thriving. I experienced so much love from family, friends, and especially from our church family for whom my husband served as minister of music and youth and interim pastor. Older friends there opened their new home to our whole family for my recovery, caregiving, and childcare. People all over the country prayed for me.

I connected with a renowned breast and thyroid specialist, a surgical oncologist, and a talented plastic surgeon. The oncologist personally did chemo in his office, administering just the right dosage so that I didn't even lose my hair. He'd compassionately held my hand while I'd been prepped for surgery.

Learning the importance of a good attitude for healing, I felt blessed and loved, and I learned to laugh through the circumstances. Chemo treatments became fun restaurant outings with whomever was driving.

If you're facing a serious diagnosis, I hope you'll accept the best medical treatment available, as well as the love and prayers from everyone willing to offer, and face survival with humor, gratitude, and courage.

*　*　*

Rose Walker also has stories published in two other CWFL's anthologies, *Mother* and *Experiencing God's Presence*, as well as the SCWC's blog. She also authored *A Mom's Mentality* and "Rose's Remuddlings."

Questions for Personal Reflection or Group Discussion

When doctors diagnosed Rose Walker with breast cancer, it plunged her into depression as she feared for her young children's future without her. Throughout her treatment, Rose received immense support from her church family and medical team. Rose's story highlights the power of community, faith, and a positive attitude in facing life-threatening illness.

Here are a few questions for personal reflection or group discussion:

1. When faced with a serious health diagnosis, what are some effective ways to manage the initial fear and uncertainty?
2. How can community and faith play a role in someone's recovery process?
3. How can someone dealing with a serious illness address the concerns of leaving family members behind, especially young children? Ponder strategies for dealing with these worries.

36

THE REDEMPTION OF EVEN THE MOST DIFFICULT DATES

BY LORAL PEPOON

My heart sank as my one of my dearest friends, Joni, called to ask if her wedding celebration date worked for me. She had asked me to be maid of honor months earlier.

"It's August 2," she said.

Really Lord?! How am I going to be maid of honor on the anniversary of my divorce? It's hard enough to still be single fifteen years later! Help!

"Of course, I'll be there," I replied, without even knowing how those words came out.

Joni and I had become dear friends once we realized our life stories were parallel. Although I was ten years older, we had both, at age twenty-seven, gotten divorced from verbally abusive men. Both of our hopes of being young wives and mothers had been shattered.

Even though I couldn't fathom how the Lord was going to get me through the wedding emotionally, I knew He would.

Within three weeks, I was on a third date with Seth, also from Nashville. We had interacted on eHarmony, an online dating site. For safety reasons, we met in a public, lovely city park, and we walked and talked, enjoying colorful wildflowers and smelling fresh honeysuckle.

Then Seth said life-changing words: "I'm a Divorce Care leader."

"I've been a Divorce Care leader too! What are the chances?"

At that moment, both of us knew God had bigger plans for us than a casual walk.

We kept dating that summer, enjoying the most relaxed relationship either of us had experienced. After Seth said "Your left hand looks naked," I invited him to Joni's wedding celebration in Grand Rapids, Ohio.

After we got to Grand Rapids on August 2, I took Seth to a sentimental place overlooking the Maumee River.

"Joni and I prayed for our future husbands on this swing during twelve weekend retreats here over the last four years, and you have every characteristic on my prayer list. I think you could be him!"

"Wow," he said with a smile.

We gazed at each other sweetly, but briefly. "I have to get to the salon to meet the bride."

At the end of the wedding celebration that evening, the fireworks in the sky matched those in my heart as I watched them with Seth.

"Let's go back to the swing," he said.

"Sure," I said.

After we got there, Seth looked serious.

"Is everything okay?" I asked.

"Sorry, I've been praying all day … I know this is the perfect place. Will you marry me?"

Seth didn't know the significance of that date, but God did. He redeems everything. August 2 went from my being divorce to my engagement anniversary.

The last ten years, married to Seth, have been the best of my life.

* * *

Author **Loral Pepoon** (loralpepoon.com) writes about God's tangible love. She penned *Clive the Cat Chimes In,* serves as managing editor of *Our Story Magazine,* and owns Selah Press Publishing.

Questions for Personal Reflection or Group Discussion

Loral Pepoon tells of her emotional journey when she is asked to be the maid of honor at a friend's wedding on the anniversary of her own painful divorce. Despite initial reservations, she commits to participating. The story beautifully illustrates themes of divine timing, healing, and redemption, culminating in a new marriage that brings Loral immense happiness and fulfillment.

Here are a few questions for personal reflection or group discussion:

1. Reflect on a time when you had to participate in a joyful event during a personal period of struggle. How did you manage your emotions, and what helped you through it?
2. Ponder how shared experiences have influenced your relationships. How can these connections provide support during difficult times?
3. What are some ways you have seen or experienced redemption in your own life? How has this changed your perspective on past events?

37

FAITHFUL LOVE

BY DEBBIE PHILLIPS

Fifteen years ago, I asked myself, "How now shall I live?" Around this time, my marriage of over twenty years ended. I liken the entire divorce experience to having one's skin filleted from one's body without the benefit of anesthesia. Ouch!

My eyes expelled water at the most inopportune moments. Often the dam of sheer resolve tried to hold back the deluge from running down my cheeks. Unfortunately, it seemed to burst minutes before a job interview. Just a side note, raccoon eyes are not a good look for one seeking employment.

I was aimless, numb, and unfocused. If I had given my attention to those feelings, I might have discovered I was mourning the loss of my family. But who had time to do that? My feet had been unexpectedly knocked out from under me, and I desperately wanted to feel the earth between my toes again. I craved something called "normal" but couldn't satisfy my longing.

Adrift for untold weeks, I went through the motions of my routine of going to church and daily Bible reading. Somehow the Lover of my soul met me at both places. He is an expert at orchestrating surprise encounters. I have since discovered He delights in wooing me. I simply didn't recognize His ways at the time.

One Wednesday evening, communion was offered at the church I was attending. I was surprised, as it is typically offered on Sundays. As the bread and wine aka grape juice were being passed, I found tears trickling down my cheeks during that tender moment as I recalled Jesus' sacrifice on the cross for me. I was also reminded of His covenant with me, much like the pledge a bride and groom make to each other in marriage.

The second meeting with my Husband (my Ish), my Maker, my God came through His Word. I had been reading through the Psalms. After reading a few passages, I began noticing two familiar words in more than one verse in those chapters. It was a light bulb moment!

Of course, I consulted with Google. Marriage topics popped up on the world's most popular search engine when I entered "faithful love" and "steadfast love" in the search bar. I was overcome with emotion. I acutely needed the answer to a question I had been asking for weeks. I deeply desired to know if the Lord and I were okay.

My promise-keeping God met me with His personal and intimate answer in the covenant of Eucharist and the covenantal promises of His faithful love in Scripture.

He passionately desires to meet you in your time of need. Ask Him about your needs. Record His answer. And share it with a friend.

* * *

Debbie Phillips began writing at the age of nine. A lifelong journaler, she developed and teaches a course on journaling. A teacher, writer, and speaker, Debbie is known for her practical wisdom, insight, and humor.

Questions for Personal Reflection or Group Discussion

Amidst the turmoil of losing a long-standing marriage, Debbie Phillips struggled with intense emotional pain and a sense of aimlessness. After a series of spiritual encounters, she found profound comfort, solace, healing, and a renewed understanding of God's steadfast love.

Here are a few questions for personal reflection or group discussion:

1. Reflect on an experience of loss in your own life. How did you cope with the immediate feelings of pain and disorientation?
2. Have you, like Debbie, ever discovered a deeper understanding of God's faithful love while reading Scripture? If so, please reflect on it.
3. Debbie mentions the importance of sharing personal experiences with others. How can sharing your struggles and insights with others aid in your healing and potentially help others?

38

HOPE FOUND IN OUR WONDERFUL COUNSELOR

BY TONY FARINELLA

*M*y older brother Mike's house was the place we went to for the holidays. Our parents and one of my brothers had passed, and Mike was the only one of us who had followed in our mother's footsteps as a culinary expert. He was an amazing cook, just like our mom had been, so it was a no-brainer to go enjoy holidays with him and his kids.

In 2015 and 2016, Mike had several health issues arise, but it was the health issues that drew him closer to God as he fought through the various doctor and hospital visits. In 2016, his health issues were bad enough that he sold his insurance business and retired at the age of fifty-two.

It was just a few days before Christmas of that year that Mike asked me to join him on a shopping trip to prepare for Christmas together. My heart leapt into my throat as he said these words:

"Tony, I am dying. After all the years of drinking, I have pretty much killed myself. I have cirrhosis, and my liver is failing. The doctors don't know how long I have left. I am giving you medical power of attorney to make decisions for me when I can't."

I agreed, and for all of 2017, I had to lean into Jesus for strength as I made medical decisions for him. In early December of 2017, I asked a pastor friend of mine to go visit Mike. He stayed with Mike all night reading Scripture to him, praying for him, and talking to him. He called me after his all-nighter with Mike to tell me about that night.

"Tony, his faith is solid. I have no doubt he belongs to Jesus."

God gave us one more Christmas with Mike, this one in the hospital where he was surrounded by loved ones. Just days after, I got the call stating that his life signs were weak, and the hospital staff wanted to know how to proceed.

Mike had shared his wishes with me—he didn't want to be kept alive on machines. On December 28 of 2017, I gave the order to remove his life support, and that night he went home to be with our mother. But more importantly, he met Jesus in Heaven.

If you have been wounded by loss of a loved one, the death of a marriage, or something similar, may I share a suggestion that helped me?

Trust in Jesus and pray for your loved ones, and one day, with God's help, you will see them again where the streets are paved with gold!

* * *

Tony Farinella is a part-time freelance content writer and a retired, disabled Army Veteran who has now returned to his love of writing stories. He lives with his wife and teenage daughter in central Missouri.

Questions for Personal Reflection or Group Discussion

In this story, Tony Farinella talks about his older brother Mike who was an accomplished cook and the family's gathering point for holidays. Mike's health deteriorates due to years of drinking, leading to cirrhosis and eventual liver failure. Before his condition worsens, Mike gives Tony medical power of attorney, entrusting him with future health decisions. Mike enjoys one last Christmas surrounded by family in the hospital. Shortly after, Tony fulfills Mike's wishes by removing him from life support, allowing him to pass peacefully.

Here are a few questions for personal reflection or group discussion:

1. Reflect on how personal crises can sometimes strengthen one's spiritual life or change one's perspective. Have you or someone you know experienced a similar transformation?
2. How do you prioritize relationships in your life, especially with those who may be facing health challenges?
3. Facing the loss of a loved one is painful experience. Tony suggests trusting in Jesus and praying for loved ones as a way to cope. What has most helped you deal with loss and grief?

39

LOVE LIFTED ME

BY JUDY DAVIS

"Hi Mom, how are you doing?" Tim asked when I picked up the phone.

"We are fine."

"Is Dad there? I have sad news. Bob has been in a serious accident. He was going to eat breakfast with a friend, and as he crossed the street, a car hit him. He is in the hospital with multiple injuries and in a coma."

After the initial shock, we called our pastor and asked for prayer for our son.

Our daughter, Cindi, had already arrived at the hospital when we arrived. When we walked into Bob's room, we both cried when we saw our broken son. Tim got there later, and when he saw his brother, he laid his head on the bed and wept.

The doctors told us he would never get any better.

After much prayer, later that week, I held my son's hand and said, "Bob, we are going to take all this off of you so you can rest."

The nurse came in later to remove the ventilator and feeding tube. We stood by his bed, holding his hand, and I quoted Psalm

23: *"The Lord is my Shepherd …. Even though I walk through the darkest valley, I will fear no evil …"*

I also read Psalm 91 and sang *"Softly and tenderly, Jesus is calling ..."* We stayed with our son until he breathed his last breath.

My sisters Beth and Sarah sent lovely gifts, a beautiful candle with words inscribed: *"Love becomes a Memory – the Memory Becomes a Treasure."* Enclosed was a sweet note: *"In loving memory of your son, Bob. May God wrap you in His arms as He holds your son in His hands …. We love you."*

The CEO of the company Bob worked for sent meals with their condolences, and a note: *"May these meals serve as a thank you for all your son did for our company. If there is anything we can do for your family, please reach out! You're in our thoughts and prayers."*

My sweet friend Ann sent a beautiful card: *"Love lifted me—when nothing else could help—love lifted me. When there are no words to feel or say ... there is the love of Jesus to comfort, and He gives peace that passes all understanding. With love, we share in your hurting hearts."*

We miss our son, but we know he is with the Lord. No more pain or suffering. We shall see him again in Heaven.

If you are wounded in a similar way, may I share a suggestion that helped me? When nothing else could help, our faith, family, friends, and love lifted us during this time of tragedy.

* * *

Judy Davis has been writing for Christian publications since 1985. Her works have been published in *God's Word for Today*, *Pathways to God*, *The Christian Pulse*, and *The Upper Room*. She completed her eighteenth book in 2020.

Questions for Personal Reflection or Group Discussion

In this story, Judy Davis talks about a heart-wrenching phone call from her son, Tim, delivering the news that Bob, his brother, had been critically injured in a car accident and was in a coma. The family, deeply shaken, gathers at the hospital where they confront the grim reality of Bob's condition. After much prayer, the family makes the painful decision to remove Bob's life support. During Bob's final moments, his mother recites Psalms and sings a hymn, providing a spiritual farewell as he passes away.

Here are a few questions for personal reflection or group discussion:

1. How do you approach making incredibly tough decisions during times of crisis? Reflect on a time when you faced a similar challenge.
2. How do spiritual beliefs and practices provide comfort in times of sorrow?
3. How do you preserve the memory of someone who has passed away? Ponder the ways in which memories can be cherished and honored.

40

LIGHT IN THE DARKNESS

BY TOMMYE LAMBERT

I wept quietly as the respiratory therapist turned off life support for my twenty-eight-year-old daughter. Tears filled my eyes, spilling onto my cheeks. I clasped Amy's lifeless hand and whispered the words of her favorite hymn into her ear.

Is God giving Amy back to me? I wondered, for she had begun squeezing my hand as I sang to her. But, with the last note, my husband said, "She is gone." The lines on the monitors were flat.

The days and weeks following Amy's death seem like a blur of one long, continuous, dark cloud. My head throbbed from constant sobbing. I wandered aimlessly around the house, spending most of my time roaming around Amy's bedroom. I read her journals and smelled her clothes. I slept in her bed and pulled hair from her brushes to touch her living DNA.

One day, I opened Amy's Bible and saw, scribbled in youthful cursive on the inside cover, words that she claimed as her life verse years ago. The Bible trembled in my hands as I recalled the two of us reading Psalm 118 for the first time. She was nine years old.

After I read verse seventeen, Amy said, "Mom, read that verse again."

I read, "I will not die, but live and proclaim what God has done."

Amy then said, "Since I am going to Heaven, I am never going to *die*. And until I do go to Heaven, I am going to notice God and proclaim what He has done."

Amy underlined Psalm 118:17 in her Bible, copied it in notebooks and journals, and posted it on her social media pages. Amy's life illustrated the verse. She became a neonatal intensive care nurse, served on mission teams, and became a spokesperson for cystic fibrosis and organ donation. Thousands attended her celebration of life service. The pastor used Psalm 118:17 as the text.

That afternoon, God used my daughter's childish scrawl and the light of His powerful Word to pierce through my dark sorrow and guide me to "live and proclaim" what He has done. I picked up the phone and called my church to resume teaching in our Wednesday night studies. I completed my DMin degree, became a patient advocate serving on national medical boards, and now manage the resource center at my church. Joy and healing have taken residence alongside my sadness, and my grief is now accompanied by life and joy.

If you have been wounded through loss, discouragement, grief, or chronic hard times, lean into God's Word. The light from His Word nurtures healing. Your path will grow brighter as you notice God and proclaim Him.

* * *

Tommye Lambert lives in Hoover Alabama. She manages The Home Front Resource Center at Hunter Street Baptist Church and is a national patient advocate. She is married to Kerry and enjoys reading, writing, and travel.

Questions for Personal Reflection or Group Discussion

Tommye Lambert tells of her profound grief and eventual healing as the mother of Amy, her twenty-eight-year-old daughter who died in young adulthood. Not long after her daughter's death, Tommye discovers a verse from Psalm 118 written in Amy's Bible, a verse that Amy had lived by. This discovery helped to rekindle Tommye's faith and propels her to re-engage with life and her community.

Here are a few questions for personal reflection or group discussion:

1. How can holding onto a loved one's belongings or revisiting shared memories serve as a bridge in processing grief?
2. How does Scripture provide comfort and guidance during times of profound grief?
3. How can one balance the experience of deep grief with the necessity or desire to engage with life again?

41

BREAKING FREE

BY DESIREE HULL

I was trapped for twenty-five years. I didn't even know a cage was forming around me. I don't remember when I lost my way. Early childhood was a time where my wings spread far and wide, but every time I experienced trauma, disappointment, or rejection, a new iron bar was formed around my heart. I thought this was protecting me, but it was encaging me slowly.

During this time, I made sure I hurt others before they had the chance to hurt me. These iron posts kept piercing my heart, one by one, post by post, forming an impenetrable layer that few, if any, could get past.

Finding my people in this darkness was impossible. Continuing to morph, with whomever I encountered, was my mask. I drowned away the person I used to, in exchange for the person the world wanted me to be, with drugs and alcohol. Lonely, abused, isolated, depressed, and riddled with anxiety, I was unrecognizable.

Staring in the mirror, I tried to decipher who I was. *Where did she go? Which layer do I peel back first to unearth the decades of hurt beneath it?*

On the beautiful summer day of June 4, 1998, I had a supernatural encounter with God. For days, I had listened to sermon after sermon, each one convicting my soul. Yearning for supernatural love and acceptance I decided to devote my life to Him. I chose to get baptized. The experience I had that day was one I would take with me for the rest of my life. It became my constant reminder that He is real, and He is with me always.

Sadly, I ran back into the world—to the place that let me down, that loved me with conditions, the world that wanted me to forget who He was, who I was. Shame, guilt, fear, and victimhood reigned over my life because it was fueled with drugs and alcohol. The wings that once made me soar were now weary and frail. I could only fly around this tiny cage for so long. I was trapped, I was wounded, I broke my own heart. Desperate, afraid, and broken, I willed myself to step into a church.

"Change or Die" was the series being preached. When the pastor said, "You have to make a slave out of your body, or your body will make a slave out of you," I felt a shift in the atmosphere. God was calling me back home, and it was time to make a change and recommit my life to Christ.

I got sober.

Now, my wings are strong, my cage is broken, and I finally fly free. Don't let addiction cage you from soaring freely with God.

* * *

Desiree Hull finds solace and healing through writing. With a heart for readers of all ages, she hopes to bring healing, hope, and transformation with her words. Visit her online at myrecoveryrevival.com.

Questions for Personal Reflection or Group Discussion

Desiree Hull traces her journey from feeling trapped in a self-made cage of emotional pain and self-destructive behaviors to a significant spiritual encounter that brings a brief period of sobriety and self-reflection. But old habits and environmental influences lead her to a relapse. Listening to a sermon, Desiree makes a choice to change, leading her on the path to recovery and spiritual renewal. Her story shows the power of God and personal courage to overcome life's addictions.

Here are a few questions for personal reflection or group discussion:

1. Desiree describes her self-built cage formed by trauma, disappointment, and rejection. Have you ever known experiences that have contributed to building walls around your own heart? If so, how did you escape and dismantle the walls?
2. Desiree knew a pivotal moment of spiritual awakening and then a painful relapse. What supports are crucial in maintaining long-term changes in life?
3. Reflect on a personal experience when you had to break free from past choices and seek a renewed sense of freedom and purpose.

42

HIS GIFTS FROM THE SEA

BY GAYLE CHILDRESS GREENE

We are at the ocean. My hair is messy and wavy with salt water, wavy like the sea. I wear a silly wide-brimmed hat. I look ridiculous, but I don't care.

My skin is kissed by the sun and scented with coconut oil. The familiar fragrance conjures days spent at the beach growing up in California. Foamy edges of waves lap at my toes, and my heels sink deeper as each wave returns to its home.

I find myself drawn here like the moon pulls the tides, where my problems are finite and my God is infinite. I feel the vastness of water and sky wrap me in an omniscient embrace, and I hear His still small voice speak to my heart, *I see you.*

I've stood on the seashore as a child, a new bride, a mother, and now, for the first time, as an empty nester. Echoes of my children's laughter dance in the wind, and my heart aches with the fresh silence of no one at home to call me *Mom.* I wipe salty tears off my face. *What now, Lord? What now?*

We have come full circle, my husband and I; back to where we started, over thirty years ago. We ride our bikes down a deserted beach. Sand shifts under our tires as we pedal against the wind, a perfect metaphor. We stop to gather shells, driftwood, and seagull feathers. The broken shells are beautiful too. I collect some as a reminder.

We discover a tide pool alive with tiny hermit crabs. I wonder how the minuscule creatures find new shells to call home as they grow. I think of my children leaving our "shell" to find their own. I pray God will guide them.

I see a tiny shrimp stranded in the sand. I scoop him up and release him into the tide pool. He vanishes into the safety of the water. Does he wonder why someone so big stooped to rescue someone so small? (It's because someone so big stooped to rescue me.)

The gentle lull of the waves at low tide coaxes me into a new rhythm, His rhythm. I try not to fight it, but rather to surrender to a new chapter, to move on ... like the hermit crab that must find a new home.

Whether it's the song of birds, a starry sky, a vast ocean, or a little hermit crab, I find solace in God's creation. It is my prayer that you will experience God's comfort in your season of life, trusting Him to write the next page.

"For everything there is a season, and a time for every matter under heaven."
(Ecclesiastes 3:1, ESV)

* * *

Gayle Childress Greene's stories are published in four previous CWFL anthologies. She is the author of *The Rat's Race* and *Because You Are Mine*, lovingly dedicated to her grandchildren who have filled her empty nest with joy.

Questions for Personal Reflection or Group Discussion

During a time of life transition to becoming an empty nester, Gayle Childress Greene revisits the ocean, a place for her of personal history and emotional significance. As she walks along the beach, she reflects on various stages of her life. Throughout her introspective journey, she finds reassurance in the small wonders of nature and in her faith, which helps her embrace the new phase of life she is encountering with a sense of peace.

Here are a few questions for personal reflection or group discussion:

1. Reflect on a natural setting that evokes deep memories for you. How does this setting influence your thoughts and feelings about your life's journey?
2. What broken or imperfect things have you found beauty or meaning in?
3. How do you approach the unknowns in your own life?

43

BURDEN BEARERS

BY NORMA WALTERS

My face crumpled as I heard the surgeon say, "We may have to amputate the leg."

Receiving a diagnosis of septic arthritis of the left knee joint, my husband had already endured five surgeries. After each operation, the surgeon repeated that same phrase. Coldness seeped into my soul each time I heard those words.

Weary and frightened, I continually cried to God. Three months later, my husband, Bill, returned home with both legs intact. But hobbling up our front steps, he lost his strength and landed face down on the cement. Firemen answered my 911 call and carried Bill into our house. I kept thinking, *God brought us this far, and He wouldn't leave us now.*

Fingers trembling, I texted my Christian friends. How was I going to transport Bill to his appointments? My six-foot-two-inch, 210-pound husband's vulnerability panicked me.

Then, God's people showed up. That night, six friends installed a five-foot ramp down our front steps. Bill navigated his wheelchair up and down that ramp for the next several months. This act of kindness turned my hopelessness into gratitude.

Administering IV antibiotics, changing wound dressings, and assisting Bill with hygiene needs were my daily tasks. I ignored the laundry piling up. One day, a friend brought two empty bags and gathered our laundry. The next day, she delivered fresh, folded laundry to our home. My friend continued this gracious act of service throughout the six months of Bill's recovery.

Focusing on Bill's care, I neglected my personal exercise. My mental and physical health suffered until women from a Christian Zumba class invited me to join. Encouragement and exercise refreshed my soul and brought health to my body. These women continue to support me to this day.

I was depleted and unable to grocery shop, and our food supply dwindled. Friends began bringing casseroles, dinners, desserts, and groceries to our home. These gifts of food were delivered daily and eased another burden off my shoulders.

Exhausted and ready to give up? I felt this way, but Christian friends shifted our burdens to their own shoulders. Bill and I were able to endure this year-long trauma because God and His people were present. God will bring solace to your soul in unimaginable ways. Trust God, and watch Him surprise you!

"Now to Him who is able to do far more abundantly beyond all that we ask or think, according to the power that works within us, to Him be the glory in the church and in
Christ Jesus to all generations forever and ever. Amen."
(Ephesians 3:20-21, NASB)

* * *

Norma Walters is a freelance writer with published stories in the Christian Writers for Life anthologies *Mother: What My Mother Taught Me About Life, Love, and Faith,* and *Experiencing God's Presence.* Follow Norma online at www.facebook.com/rchs/walters.

Questions for Personal Reflection or Group Discussion

Norma Walters writes about a time when she and her husband faced a severe medical crisis—septic arthritis in her husband's knee. The doctor threatened amputation after multiple surgeries. During this time, Norma cared for her husband. The couple received overwhelming support from members of their community—a newly-built front door ramp, delivered meals, and laundry services. Norma story shows the power of love and community, and the unexpected ways their kind support provided strength and hope as the couple faced troublesome challenges.

Here are a few questions for personal reflection or group discussion:

1. Reflect on a time when you or a loved one faced a health scare or another kind of crisis. How did you manage your fear and uncertainty?
2. Ponder the impact of acts of kindness during difficult times. Can you recall a moment when loved ones helped you during a crisis? What lessons did you learn?
3. Say aloud Ephesians 3:20-21 and ponder its meaning. What do these verses say to you when you face personal challenges and unexpected crises?

44

IN HIS HAND

BY FLORA REIGADA

As we drove to the hospital that December night, with a nip in the air and homes glittering with decorations, we never imagined the trouble facing us.

My husband had been slurring his words and making no sense. As a precaution, our son had offered to drive us. Because Dan had since returned to normal, there was no sense of urgency.

A calm doctor greeted us in the emergency room, and I explained what had happened.

His demeanor never changed as he said, "I'm going to light a fire."

The doctor must have pressed a button because young people pushing equipment and holding devices ran from every direction. Dan was soon on a gurney, hooked up to IVs and beeping equipment.

How could this vulnerable, strapped-down man possibly be my strong, capable husband?

"He's having a stroke," someone said. The words stabbed at my heart. Dan was admitted to the hospital for a few days of tests.

"He needs heart valve replacement surgery," a cardiologist soon informed me.

A screaming ambulance rushed Dan to another hospital where a renowned heart surgeon would perform the surgery.

When the day came, our son and I were directed to a waiting room to join a tense vigil of waiting loved ones. My prayers were short and desperate.

Lord, help Dan. Guide the surgeon's hand. I held my breath when the surgeon entered the room and walked to us.

"We replaced two valves—aortic and mitral. Everything went well."

Seeing Dan being wheeled down the hall on a gurney, intubated but alive, I could finally breathe.

He was brought to the ICU where he was confronted by a cacophony of beeping and flashing equipment, with bright lights reflected in glass partitions and a continuous parade of doctors and nurses.

We held our breath while Dan opened his eyes, looked around and whispered our names. Later he demanded, "Why are dogs and toys in the hall?"

I peeked out, expecting representatives from Therapy Dogs or Toys for Tots, but I saw only hospital staff.

Dan began punching at nurses and had to be restrained. "He's in a postoperative delirium," a nurse told me.

Over the next week, the confusion melted into tears of gratitude, and Dan thought back. "During my surgery, I heard a voice say, 'Your heart is in my hand and I want you to live.'" We wondered if Dan had heard the doctor, or if he had heard Jesus, the Great Physician.

As Dan and I navigate life's challenges such as aging, it helps us to remember that the Great Physician holds our heart in His hand. Your heart is there too, forever secure. You can always trust the Great Physician.

* * *

Flora Reigada is an award-winning journalist and novelist, writing for *Senior Life Newspaper* and Miller Words Books. Look for her inspirational thriller, *Bibles and Bones in the Forest*, coming soon from Miller Words. Visit Flora online at FloraReigada.blogspot.com.

Questions for Personal Reflection or Group Discussion

When Flora Reigada's husband, Dan, has alarming symptoms, Flora and her son drive Dan to the hospital. The hospital staff spring into action after realizing Dan is having a stroke, and they prepare him for heart valve replacement surgery. The surgery is successful, but Dan experiences postoperative delirium, causing confusion and distress. In the midst of this turmoil, Dan shares a profound experience of hearing a reassuring voice during surgery, which he interprets as divine reassurance.

Here are a few questions for personal reflection or group discussion:

1. Reflect on a time when an unexpected event disrupted a generally happy or calm time in your life. How did you manage the sudden shift in circumstances?
2. Ponder the emotional impact of seeing a loved one in a weakened state. How can this change your perception of strength and vulnerability?
3. Reflect on how faith can play a role in coping with life's challenges, especially health issues.

45

BREATHE

BY KATHY STEPHENS BOWEN

The vacuum sound of the emergency room doors led to the pounding of feet. It was like a stampede of wild horses vibrating the floor, my husband on a gurney. A blurred vision remains of that horrific moment of him in a full-blown code. *Breathe…*

I watched intently their every move, but my insides were screaming. *"Can't you see that he is dead?"*

Breathe…

I was forced back into the waiting room. TICK TOCK, TICK TOCK was the sound of the clock. I found myself rocking back and forth to soothe my soul.

Abruptly, three doctors appeared. My heartbeat became louder than their voices, but I could see their lips moving. Their next words were deafening. "Mrs. Stephens, we are so sorry but there was nothing we could do." *Breathe…*

Everything I knew about life changed in that moment. Dennis was the love of my life for twenty-three years. He had become my game changer. Dennis taught me about true love and absolute trust.

That night in the ER became the most pivotal day of my life.

Pivotal means to change course, reset, shift, or re-establish. Pivotal moments come in the middle of loss, disappointment, rejection, bad choices, abuse ... and many more times. They say we grow from pivotal moments.

The aftermath was a *do or die* moment.

Weeks after Dennis's death, I found myself numb, and prayer seemed unattainable. I was crouched in a valley of despair, hopeless and confused.

Late one Sunday afternoon, I found myself face down in our bed. I pulled his pillow close to my chest, and what began as an uncontrollable sob turned into a desperate cry for help.

God, please help me! I can't breathe.

I remember the deep pain as I wept. I'm not sure how long I laid there, but God met me in that place. The Holy Spirit began ministering to my spirit. His presence was indescribable. I felt the Holy Spirit say, *Let go of the pain and anguish and depend on the One who knows your every need.* On that day, God took something so broken and began to mold it into something beautiful.

Breathe.

The tapestry in our lives is woven by the pivotal moments we survive. God isn't surprised by what we endure. He is waiting for us to lean into Him and totally surrender.

My worst nightmare has become my greatest walk with God.

Your story isn't over, and my story isn't over. God still has a purpose and a plan for each of our lives.

What you know about Christ matters. But *who you are in Christ* matters most. *Breathe.*

"He heals the brokenhearted and bandages their wounds" (Psalm 147:3).

* * *

Kathy Stephens Bowen finds peace in prayer and inner healing work that can move people to hope in Christ. She is a Certified Health Coach and Christian Life Coach. She is a Certified Yoga Instructor. She uses these tools to help others be their best.

Questions for Personal Reflection or Group Discussion

Kathy Stephens Bowen writes about a deeply traumatic moment in her life. Her husband, Dennis, undergoes a medical emergency and tragically dies despite the frantic efforts of the emergency room staff. The event leaves Kathy grappling with the stark reality of her husband's death. In the aftermath of his death, Kathy descends into a valley of despair, feeling numb and disconnected from prayer. She reaches a turning point, however, when she surrenders her grief to God.

Here are a few questions for personal reflection or group discussion:

1. Kathy talks about letting go of pain and depending on God. Ponder the concept of surrender in the context of personal trials. What does surrender look like to you, and how can it aid in healing?
2. Reflect on the statement, "Your story isn't over, and my story isn't over." How does this perspective affect your approach to future challenges and opportunities?
3. How does the sudden loss of a loved one alter your understanding of life and relationships?

46

RESTORED FOR MORE

BY ABIGAIL RAYN

Broken heart syndrome (also known as stress cardiomyopathy) may occur due to severe grief and can even mimic a heart attack. I didn't understand this, or panic attacks, until I became a grandma without grandchildren.

I thought things would just blow over and I would soon see my grandchildren again. But weeks turned into months, and months soon turned into years.

Shopping for gifts triggered panic attacks. Then came the day when a package was delivered with "RETURN TO SENDER" stamped in bold red letters, followed by a text message requesting no more packages.

My world collapsed. The mere sight of children was suffocating. The pain of being a grandparent without grandchildren was more than I could bear. How could I go on living while watching friends with children and grandchildren enjoying holidays with their families? It became excruciating for me to listen to their stories and try to be happy for them.

My counselor explained the notion of "ambiguous grieving." Grieving someone who is still alive is even harder than grieving the death of a loved one because it is perpetual.

Now, my feelings had a name. Closure would be elusive, but adapting might be possible. I was then faced with a decision—to continue living in this state of mourning forever, or to learn to live and love again, though with a broken heart.

I knew God had better plans for me. Therefore, I would need to learn how to navigate uncharted waters of living with an estranged family, depending on God daily for strength and guidance.

I woke from my spiritual coma with a feeling of renewed urgency and asked God to restore my joy and His calling on my life. But how does one go on living without a vital body part, like an organ or limb? When a loved one is gone, a real part of you is missing. Nothing can fill the void or replace them. Only God can!

When I released my broken heart to Him, He replaced my genetic grandchildren with spiritual grandchildren. He blessed me with the opportunity to work with adults living with dementia. They have such a childlike love for everything, including Him! I am so grateful that I get to walk with them in this journey as they draw near to the end of their earthly lives.

Are you living estranged from loved ones? Release it to your Heavenly Father and know that He has a plan for you. A plan to prosper, not for harm. As He did for Job, He will restore. "After Job had prayed for his friends, the Lord restored his fortunes and gave him twice as much as he had before" (Job 42:10 NIV).

* * *

Abigail Rayn is a published author, COTA (Certified Occupational Therapy Assistant), and Dementia Care Specialist. Her writing is an insight and reflection of life through a lens of faith. Read more at www.walkingwithrayn.com.

Questions for Personal Reflection or Group Discussion

In this story, Abigail Rayn, a grandmother, struggles with the heartache of being separated from her grandchildren. This profound grief triggers severe emotional responses, including stress cardiomyopathy, commonly known as broken heart syndrome, and panic attacks when faced with reminders of her grandchildren. Choosing to embrace life, she turns to her faith for strength and guidance, asking God to restore her joy and purpose.

Here are a few questions for personal reflection or group discussion:

1. Have you ever experienced a form of grief for someone still alive, such as through estrangement or divorce? How does this type of grief differ from mourning a death, and how have you coped with it?
2. How can faith provide comfort and guidance during times of deep emotional pain? Ponder a personal experience where your faith played a crucial role in your healing.
3. Ponder the importance of seeking professional help, such as counseling, during times of severe emotional distress. What role do support systems play in helping someone navigate through intense grief or depression?

47

HOPE COMES IN HEALING

BY SUSAN SHUMWAY

I walked out of the courthouse feeling no emotion except a quiet sigh of exhausted relief. There were no high-fives or celebrations planned; instead, it was more the stark reality that my marriage was over.

You may tell me you are sorry, and thank you. But I was the one to end the marriage. I had been in an emotionally abusive and destructive marriage for thirty-nine years. The courtroom was simply the place where it was legally terminated.

Now, I need to take the pieces of my wounded heart and try to put them all back together. I felt as though someone had precariously dropped all five thousand pieces at my feet. Some of the pieces are completely white, and some are black, so where do I even begin? I am weary from the fight. Were the last thirty-nine years of my life wasted?

God hates divorce. So do I. God called me to do my very best, and I did until I knew it was time to walk away from this unhealthy relationship. The unchanging toxic environment was depleting the very life from me, and I knew what I must do to save me.

It has now been four years, and it certainly wasn't the easy way out, that is for sure. But I also want to say that God was bigger than all the mountains I had to climb. My valleys were so deep that, many days, the sun refused to appear. But God has never failed me, and He has given me time to reflect and grow in Him.

I am not the same person who walked out of the courthouse that day. God has given me peace that I did the right thing, and He has provided for me in ways that I never dreamed possible—and in greater abundance than I ever imagined.

This morning, I sit in church with my ex-husband for a musical program for our grandchildren. No, we are not getting back together. But I have no hatred. There is no animosity. Instead, I sit there in awe of the mighty God I serve, and the way He has changed me and given me a love and a peace that I can't describe.

The thirty-nine years were not in vain. God gave us two amazing children I refer to as the *trophies of God's grace*. We have six beautiful grandchildren, two of whom brought us together today, so I can say, God can use every circumstance of our lives for His glory. God can take our sins and mistakes and bring us closer to Him. My wounded heart beats again, and He brings great hope in my life.

* * *

Susan Shumway is a published author of *The Long Road Back to Me* and a *Guideposts* contributor. She has also been published in previous CWFL anthologies and other devotionals. Writing is her joy.

Questions for Personal Reflection or Group Discussion

Susan Shumway shares her personal journey of a thirty-nine-year emotionally abusive marriage. She makes the difficult decision to divorce and walks out of the courthouse feeling a mixture of relief and daunting uncertainty about her future. Over time, God provides peace and new opportunities, allowing her to rebuild a life filled with greater self-understanding and harmony. She shows that even deeply painful experiences can contribute to personal growth and spiritual depth.

Here are a few questions for personal reflection or group discussion:

1. Reflect on a time when ending a difficult situation also meant facing a new set of challenges. How did you navigate that transition?
2. Ponder how difficult experiences can sometimes lead to significant personal or spiritual growth.
3. How important is forgiveness or reconciliation in healing from past wounds? Is it always possible or desirable?

48

MY LAST DAY?

BY SUSAN BERG HEEG

"You're lucky to be alive," said the hematologist.

I looked at the pictures as he scrolled through my scans, one after another. There were more clots in my lungs than I could count.

"I'll put you on blood thinners for six months. In that time, your body should have dissolved them. Then we'll keep track of future clots with a test called the D-dimer. It indicates another clot."

I knew in my spirit that God was in charge. For weeks before this, I had huffed and puffed as I walked. But on this day, as I walked into church for Bible study, I stopped halfway across the parking lot. I couldn't breathe or walk. I felt like all the energy had evaporated from my body.

Usually no one was at the church door on Monday mornings. However, that day, God placed three men there to fix the door. When they saw me pause, they came running. One man took me home where we called the ambulance while the others brought my car home and notified my Bible study members. They began to pray.

In the ambulance, I worried about my low oxygen. After

receiving the diagnosis at the hospital, I experienced tremendous fear. But God is good. Over time and through prayers, I felt God's peace. He saved me for a purpose. What would it be?

The six months rolled on, and I began writing a book about God's deep-down hope, peace, and joy amidst life's difficulties. Had I not just learned this, along with many other lessons in my life, through trials? One year later, my book to turn eyes to Jesus was published.

Next, God turned me to my grandchildren and gave me a great desire to understand the Gen Z generation (ages fourteen to twenty-six). God dropped young people into my path, and I invited them to talk about what life was like for them. I hope to bless grandparents with ideas to understand and help God's wonderful young people.

However, a new spin recently surfaced when my D-dimer, the test to find evidence of blood clots, was very high. Fear—there it was again. More clots?

The doctor said the test probably wasn't a good one for me, because my other inflammation can also trigger it. I wasn't happy with that answer and the decision to conduct no further tests. So, I wait.

But God! That night, as I was praying, peace settled over me. Spiritual joy!

If you are weary in living with fear of the unknown, may I share God's reminder to me? Live each day as if it is your last. Work out God's purpose for you in focusing on and loving God and other people. This will bring true peace!

***

Susan Berg Heeg is an award-winning author/speaker. Her latest book, *God's Song in Your Soul: Keys to Finding Joy in the Midst of Difficulties,* is available on Amazon or on her website, susanbergheeg.com.

Questions for Personal Reflection or Group Discussion

Susan Berg Heeg begins her story with receiving a critical health diagnosis from a hematologist—a life-threatening condition. Susan credits her survival to God's divine intervention, which reinforces her faith. Susan finds peace through prayer and a resolve to live each day fully, focusing on God's purpose, helping others, and spreading love.

Here are a few questions for personal reflection or group discussion:

1. How have life's trials helped you discover or reaffirm your purpose in God's work? Ponder examples of how challenges have shaped your life's direction.
2. Why is it important to understand and connect with different generations? Ponder ways you can or have bridged generational gaps within your own family or community.
3. How do you find peace and maintain hope while living with ongoing health concerns or uncertainty about the future? How does your faith in God give you strength and hope?

MY DUCK OF GRACE

BY SUSAN STEDMAN

In 2007, my family and my sister's family helped my grandmother move into a new house. We worked all day packing, loading, unloading, and unpacking, and we left for the hour-and-a-half drive home well after dark.

We were all exhausted and stopped at a small restaurant for dinner. On the way out, the kids noticed a gumball machine that was filled with tiny rubber ducks and duck tattoos. We obviously weren't thinking straight by that time because my husband started pumping quarters into the machine, trying to win all four of the over-eighteen "kids" a rubber duck. However, after nearly ten dollars in quarters, they all had handfuls of tattoos but no rubber ducks.

I was the last one out, and I had fifty cents, so I tried my hand. I even said a prayer, for some reason. *God, I really want a duck.* I put the money in, turned the handle, and a tiny, yellow-spotted duck fell into my hand. I was elated and ran outside showing off my duck.

It didn't occur to me till the next morning that I had probably been silly and irresponsible to pray to God for a rubber duck. I apologized to Him and told Him that I didn't mean it in any bad way. I didn't know why I even did it. I was so used to praying constantly that I guess I just did it out of habit.

While I was praying that morning, I understood that God was not upset with me. He asked me if I knew why He had answered my prayer. I had no guess, so He told me.

Because I want you to know that I am not like your earthly father. When you ask something of me, I will not let you down. I want you to know that you can trust me to give you good things.

I started to cry because I could feel those words even more than I could hear them. My birth father was not a man whom I could trust or believe. He was addicted to drugs from before I was born until he died in 2013. There's more, but I will leave it at that.

Many people have been let down by their parents, and it affects the way they perceive a relationship with God. Don't be afraid to ask Him for help learning to trust Him. His ways are beautiful.

I still have my "duck of grace." It sits in my basket beside my bed. He is seventeen years old this year.

* * *

Susan Stedman started writing stories when she was six and never stopped. She has seven published novels about clean and/or Christian romance. You can find her on Amazon.

Questions for Personal Reflection or Group Discussion

Susan Stedman shares a story that happened in 2007 after a long day of helping her grandmother move. At a restaurant, she whimsically prays for a rubber duck from a gumball machine—a prayer that is unexpectedly answered. This small event led to a profound spiritual revelation in Susan's life, deepening her understanding of God's nature.

Here are a few questions for personal reflection or group discussion:

1. Reflect on a time when a small or unexpected event brought about deep insight or a change in your perspective.
2. Ponder how negative experiences with earthly relationships can influence one's view of God. How have personal relationships in your own life shaped your understanding of trust and faith?
3. Do you have any physical objects that serve as spiritual or emotional reminders for you? What are they, and what do they represent in your life?

50

HE'S ON TIME

BY JANET SHEARER

The music thundered from the nearby SUV. I nodded my head in rhythm with the beat as I escorted my mother-in-law through the grocery store parking lot and to the passenger's side door of my own car. Mom advanced in spurts, and I reminded myself to be patient.

"They're playing some good music," I commented, hoping Mom would respond. She held the fresh flower bouquet we had bought to brighten her kitchen counter during the coming storm. Both a week-long hard freeze and Valentine's Day were fast approaching. In the store, I had steered her past the candy bouquets to select blossoms of deep red.

My in-laws had been married fifty-eight years. They never were much for celebrating Valentine's Day. Who needs a trivial holiday when you have the never-dying kind of love?

Dying. Dad was dying. Acute myeloid leukemia raged through his bloodstream. I was not sure how much of that Mom understood. Dementia was meticulously taking the younger, more vibrant version of her.

As Mom climbed into the car, a lyric from the blaring music reached my ears. *"He's on time. He's on time,"* came the call and response from the gospel tune. The truth pouring from the neighboring vehicle calmed my questioning, burdened soul.

On top of the pandemic we were a year into, the last six weeks had been filled with nights in the hospital, days in the chemotherapy center, then seizures, MRIs, blood transfusions, dizziness, and coughing spells. Friends and family stayed with Mom while my husband worked. I cared for Dad and attempted to keep up with my job duties. Just a few days earlier, we had begun making arrangements for a paid sitter.

Who knew if the sitter would work out? Who knew how many nights my husband and I would spend in his parents' home? Who knew how long we would need to juggle schedules? Who knew if Dad's blood cells would respond to treatment? Who knew?

God knew. He's on time.

Hadn't I witnessed His timing already? My husband and his brother, states away, struggled with approaching Dad about help for caregiving. On the road to the fifth day of chemotherapy, and in the wake of countless prayers, Dad looked at me and said, "You can't keep doing all this." It was the opening I needed.

Yet, how quickly I forget, and how often I need to be reminded. Perhaps you need a reminder too. Keep praying and looking to God for the answers, the small signs of His hand at work in your life. God knows, and He is on time . . . with a sitter, with a song, with whatever you need during stormy days.

* * *

Janet Shearer is a Mississippi writer and artist documenting and painting a creative life. She and her husband, Dale, have two children, a ballerina and a filmmaker. Janet's work can be found at janetdshearer.com.

Questions for Personal Reflection or Group Discussion

Janet Shearer shares a poignant story built on themes of faith in God, the challenges of caregiving, and the solace found in small, meaningful signs during life's most turbulent times.

Here are a few questions for personal reflection or group discussion:

1. Janet finds solace in a song lyric that reassures her of God's divine timing. Reflect on a moment when a message, whether through music, a conversation, or a sign, provided you with timely comfort or guidance. How did it impact your feelings or decisions at that time?
2. Ponder the emotional and practical challenges of caregiving. How do you balance compassion with personal well-being?
3. How does your faith in God help you navigate uncertain or difficult times? Can you recall a specific instance where you felt guided or supported by your faith? Reflect on the details of that instance.

HOPE OVERCOMES GRIEF

BY DIANNE J. RICHARDSON

Where do I start, God? How can I do this? Silence, only deathly silence.

Cerise, paper-like bougainvillea blossoms were striking against the ink blue sea and stark against brilliant, whitewashed walls and blue domes of the Grecian clifftops. My eyes closed, a gentle sea breeze kissing my cheeks. The searing hot sun baked on my arms. Disembarking the cruise from Crete, I was lost in my forest of reflection.

Days before, the phone's shrill ring cut the air. My husband answered: "Hello?" Seconds later, he was standing in front of me, expressionless. "She is here. I'll pass her the phone."

Have you ever felt your thunderous heart? My brother lives abroad. We rarely spoke on the phone as overseas calls were expensive. "Hello, John. What a lovely surprise! How are you?"

"Dianne, I am so sorry …." A pause, then his broken voice continued. "I have really bad news. Dad died earlier today following a massive heart attack. Dad is dead!"

Slowly, I climbed the steep stone steps winding their way into the hillside. I was still in shock, numb with pain and looking for comfort as I stood inside the small cave church.

Inside the humble structure of this tiny place of worship, I noticed faded icons. A single, ornately designed bronze lampstand held burning candles, casting a soft light and lengthy shadows against the dark interior of the cave.

I tentatively reached for a candle and lit it, saying my first prayer for my father, warm tears rolling down my cheeks. This was the first acknowledgement that he was no longer alive.

The warm light emitted by the candle represented hope for me. I knew my father was now clothed in an eternal light. Standing at his open grave the week before, I had a vision of a golden chalice being taken up a golden flight of stairs, stairs that led into the heavens. I could not look into the bright light. I could only focus on the golden staircase and the warm peace bathing and cloaking me.

Have you have lost a loved one, felt the raw, emotional talons clawing and ripping out your heart? Grief doesn't ever leave you, but it takes on different meaning over time.

My realization, through a vision at my father's grave, is that when someone you love dies, there is hope—a hope in knowing we will be reunited with them in God's eternal kingdom. Death is not the end.

Do you consider your own mortality? Have you asked *that* big question, *What happens when I die?* Many see death as a taboo subject. *But, we all have* hope. God transformed me by His abundant grace, forgiveness, and love, and He holds the same for you. Death has lost its sting and power. Will you welcome God in?

* * *

Dianne J. Richardson, author of *Hope Reigns*, is no stranger to overcoming various trials in life. By receiving God's love, her mission is making a difference in the lives of others through encouragement and sharing faith.

Questions for Personal Reflection or Group Discussion

Dianne J. Richardson begins her story as she experiences a profound moment of silence and reflection in the Greek islands after receiving the devastating news that her father had suddenly died due to a heart attack. The story explores themes of loss, the inevitability of death, and the power of faith. It concludes with an invitation to reflect on mortality and the comfort of God's promises.

Here are a few questions for personal reflection or group discussion:

1. The candle in the cave church is a powerful symbol of hope. Reflect on a time when a simple act or object helped you find hope during a difficult period.
2. Why do you think death is often seen as a taboo subject, and how can opening up about it help us find peace?
3. Dianne's faith in God plays a crucial role in her healing. How do you think a deep faith can aid in coping with loss and grief?

52

THE PROMISE

BY LISA A. DENUNZIO-GOMES

"*I* will destroy everything you think you know about Christianity. But I promise to give it back to you better than you ever thought it could be." The dean of philosophy at my university in New York had offered the warning to his students in his Christianity class on the very first day.

After he announced his intent, I pretty much forgot his heady remarks; however confident, they seemed more like an overzealous guarantee to me. I did not record his warning in my notes. His opening remarks did not strike me as super-relevant, like he would sneak them into one of his notoriously complex exams while his promise evaporated quickly. They were forgettable because, for the most part, the word *promise* is an airless accent piece, only meant to accessorize a plotline. Promises yield nothing in reality. They're just words.

The glaring F I received on my midterm paper, and my overall grade of C+, were a blow to a born and raised Roman Catholic. My paper was so bad that I'd won the honor of the professor personally giving me my grades and then recommending that I opt out of his two advanced classes on immortality and eternity and Christian mysticism.

Receiving word of my failure was a humiliating experience. Right there in his office, I found myself unable to control a wide range of emotions. My embarrassment gave his assessment credibility—if he said I am a failure, then I must be.

Retreat seemed like the only logical choice to recover some dignity, but in retreating, I risked facing embarrassment again. So, semesters later, I walked back into his classroom. Win, lose, or draw, I would strive toward an unknown and intangible reward.

The A grades I received in both of his advanced classes are counted as achievements that are relative to my utter failure. But also, the high marks gave substance to my professor's promise from two years earlier. The C+ I received was proof that he did, indeed, destroy all I thought I knew about Christianity, and he did so without my consent. But the A grades proved I received something even better.

However, I must not think that those grades mean I know squat about Christianity. Those grades simply reflect how I grasped his version of the topic, and just because I aced his classes does not mean *he* knows squat about Christianity. Neither my grades nor the elation substantiating his promise is the reason why I trust that his version is the closest to the truth.

I believe because I have come to see that what is true about God cannot be destroyed. Instead, only the fabrications, fantasies, and myths will shatter and evaporate into airlessness.

* * *

Lisa A. DeNunzio-Gomes has completed several Christian fiction novels that explore healthy faith practices with the theme that heroes, love, and magic are only real, true, and good through God. She is actively seeking representation.

Questions for Personal Reflection or Group Discussion

Lisa A. DeNunzio-Gomes, a Roman Catholic university student, tells the story of her professor, a dean who boldly promised to revolutionize Lisa's understanding of Christianity and to destroy everything the students think they know about Christianity. Lisa excels in the advanced courses and later comes to the understanding that genuine faith and truth about God cannot be destroyed.

Here are a few questions for personal reflection or group discussion:

1. Have you ever had your beliefs seriously challenged by someone else's perspective? How did you respond, and what was the outcome?
2. How do grades or formal evaluations influence your perception of your own knowledge and abilities? Can these always be trusted to accurately reflect your understanding or potential? Why or why not?
3. How do you reconcile academic knowledge with personal faith or belief?

53

MY ANGEL WEARS PEARLS

BY TERESA NEWTON-TERRES

I awoke and headed to bathe in the sunrise and seaside. My heart was heavy with despair because of recent journeys from my home by one sea to my mother's across the sea. Mother's health was declining.

As I gazed across the crystal waters, a woman dressed in white linen paused beside me. Pearls encircled her neck.

"Elegant," I said.

"Pearls are so spiritual," she said. Her Scandinavian accent soothed my soul.

"Spiritual?" My eyes encircled her iridescent spheres.

"Just think of the oyster." She raised a cupped palm like an oyster. "How irritating to have a grain of sand inside." Her fingers touched the center and encircled her oyster as if to represent layers building. "Over time, the oyster placed layers around the irritation to create a pearl. Likewise, layers of *love*, encircling our life's irritations, will create a *pearl* for our *heart*."

I said nothing as I began to walk beside Annie. I spilled out my heart's sorrow, how I had returned from being by my mother's bedside. I was doing my best, yet my best seemed not enough.

Mother had always seemed independent; now, she was dependent on others. By the end of this recent visit, my mother could not get out of bed, and conversations were shallow.

I grappled with what to do for my mother, and how to attend to my family and run a business.

Annie listened.

Then, she stopped and laid a gentle hand on mine. "When you have done all you can do, you can pray, knowing that God will send His angels to meet all needs. You don't know what form an angel will take, but you can rest *knowing* God sends the right angel at just the right time."

I nodded as tears spilled onto my cheeks.

We continued walking and returned to where we began.

Annie fondled her pearls. "These are pop beads," she began. "A gift from my grandson who saved his pennies for these pearls." Annie continued, "May angels comfort your mother and you to build pearls."

I never saw my mother again, as she died before my next journey to her bedside.

When I returned to the nursing facility to gather Mother's belongings, my heart was encircled by layers of love as I realized that, in Mother's convalescence, she had angels—her family had traveled great distances to remind her of fond memories. Since Mother had retired from that same nursing facility, the staff honored her with gracious financial discounts, showered her with flowers, lovingly held her hand, and prayed during her final moments.

Mother experienced angels, and I experienced one wearing plastic pearls.

Take irritations upon your heart, surround them with layers of love, and transform them into treasures.

* * *

Teresa Newton-Terres is the award-winning author, with James Pence, of the *Mystery of the Marie*, a memoir of how her childhood tragedy surfaced a Cold War secret. Follow her at www.TnewtonT.com.

Questions for Personal Reflection or Group Discussion

As Teresa Newton-Terres struggles with the emotional weight of a sick mother, walking by the sea she encounters a woman wearing pearls named Annie. Engaging in conversation, Annie gives Teresa a new perspective on handling life's challenges.

Here are a few questions for personal reflection or group discussion:

1. What does Annie tell Teresa about pearls and life's irritations? Reflect on a personal irritation or challenge you've faced. How can you apply the metaphor of the pearl to your situation?
2. What does Annie tell Teresa about prayer and trust in God's interventions?
3. Have you ever received help or support from an unexpected source at a crucial moment? Ponder that encounter and its impact on your life.

54

THREE LAYERS OF GRIEF

BY RHONDA MOORE

The morning after Thanksgiving of 2019, my sister called our mama. She had been sick that week. Mama wasn't speaking plainly, and my sister recognized that Mama was having a stroke.

After a full day, Mama was transferred from our local hospital to a larger hospital. Doctors ran tests and asked many questions. Mama's speech was completely garbled; we couldn't understand the words she spoke.

Dad was a severe diabetic, and we soon discovered Mama had kept him going. It became necessary to place Mama in a nursing home in early 2020. With Daddy's blood sugar constantly fluctuating, he could barely function alone.

One weekend, Dad called my brother. Dad was very ill and needed the hospital. With a blockage in his intestine, surgery was necessary. Dad spent over a month hospitalized.

Dad needed rehab just as Covid hit the United States. Mama's nursing facility was no longer accepting new patients, so we were forced to place him in another facility. We were afraid that he and Mama would never see each other again.

In October, we were able to place Dad into the facility with

Mama. With his many health concerns, we were forced to place him on hospice as the only way for them to be together.

On December 23, we received the call. Daddy was dying. I drove with tears streaming. Before I arrived, he passed, with Mama by his side. With broken hearts, we carried Mama home.

Another storm blew in July 2021 when a tumor was found in our disabled daughter's breast. A surgeon confirmed cancer, the worst kind. Her multiple health problems made her unable to undergo months of strong chemo. Her life would be shortened if we treated her. In August 2022, we said goodbye to our precious girl.

I tried to prepare for her death. At first, I felt numb. Alone, I cried out to God for help.

I decided to attend GriefShare, and I also received counseling provided by for pastor's families.

GriefShare was good for me. Learning the stages of grief and sharing openly with others brought a measure of relief. Four others in our group shared the same pain of losing a child.

In February of 2023, Mama passed away in her bedroom. Five of her children stood around her bed as she went home with the Lord.

Today, I lean on God for His strength. I am comforted by His presence and His Word. I run to Him when I'm overwhelmed. Church and family are a strong support, but God understands like no one else. If you find yourself on this journey of grief, asking God for help is a first step toward healing.

* * *

Rhonda Moore, a pastor's wife for thirty-eight years, has served in various positions and is now a pianist. She is mother to two sons and was blessed to be a full-time caregiver for her daughter.

Questions for Personal Reflection or Group Discussion

Rhonda Moore recounts a series of family tragedies that began the day after Thanksgiving of 2019. Amid these challenges, Rhonda relies heavily on her faith, grief support groups, and the counsel of her church. She finds solace in the community and God's support as she navigates the painful journey of grief and loss.

Here are a few questions for personal reflection or group discussion:

1. Reflect on a time when you faced multiple challenges or losses. How did you manage the stress and emotions associated with these events?
2. How have support systems helped you, or someone you know, in times of grief or crisis? What made these supports helpful and comforting?
3. How does spiritual and personal belief play a role in your coping mechanisms during difficult times? How do you depend on faith in God when you face challenging and painful crises?

55

A POINSETTIA FOR CHRISTMAS

BY SHARON ROSE GIBSON

I gazed at the crumpled, artificial poinsettia in the corner by the little refrigerator in my bedroom.

My heart sank. *I've been in this small room for three years now, and I can't even put up my Christmas tree with my favorite ornaments.*

Three years prior to this, my husband decided he didn't want to live with me. He had other love interests. Although I certainly was less than perfect, it wasn't my choice. Because of the financial decisions he made, which ended in bankruptcy, I had to move in with friends.

I had decorated the year I moved, and again the subsequent year, but this year I could not bring myself to do much. With reduced energy and resources, it took all I had to take care of myself.

As I grieved my present situation, I had little hope. At my age, in my senior years, I moved more slowly, without the energy of youth. It was harder to do normal things quickly. Yet I needed to figure out how to continue to support myself.

As I contemplated my situation. I felt more grief than joy. I spent long hours in my room, wrestling with my thoughts, seeking God and His wisdom.

As I did, the normal material joys of Christmas faded. I experienced an intimacy with God in my suffering. Christmas, after all, did not begin with shopping for gifts, decorated houses, and parties.

Christ was born into suffering and came to suffer. He's glad I know Him and can turn to Him for comfort. That's why He came—to be there for me and to redeem what the enemy stole from me.

To my surprise, someone sent me some money through the church. Later, a friend gave me money. My aunt sent a gift. An older pastor at our church came up to me: "You have a poinsettia out in the lobby for you."

I went out, and on the table sat a large, beautiful poinsettia, bigger than any I had ever had. My Bridegroom King made sure I received one!

After I picked up the check and the poinsettia, I sat in the car for a long time, contemplating His goodness to me. Tears came. He is my husband now, and He heals my wounded heart.

I had gifts, and I gave gifts. I had money to spend and a new level of intimacy in the fellowship of Jesus' sufferings.

As I gazed at the crumpled poinsettia in the corner, and now at the fresh, big, beautiful one, it reminded me that God restored to me better than before.

God doesn't have favorites. What He did for me, He can do for you.

* * *

Sharon Rose Gibson has a passion to equip you to "Write Your Story NOW" at 15minutewriter.com. She's written several books on writing and sharing your stories. Sharon grew up in Africa and has adopted seven teenagers.

Questions for Personal Reflection or Group Discussion

In this story, Sharon Rose Gibson reflects on her challenging circumstances following a painful divorce that leaves her financial unstable and in emotional distress. She grieves and feels lonely. But she also experiences a profound spiritual intimacy with God. This story shows one faithful woman's resilience, spiritual growth, and the power of community and divine love in the face of personal adversity.

Here are a few questions for personal reflection or group discussion:

1. How has a personal adversity impacted your spiritual journey? What did you discover about yourself and your faith in God?
2. Reflect on the role of community in healing from personal wounds.
3. Have you ever experienced a similar transformation in your life? Ponder the circumstances.

56

COURAGE TO LIVE A MEANINGFUL LIFE

BY ANDY BUI

*R*aised in a Buddhist home as a Catholic Christian, my apathy toward religion was apparent as I grew up quite confused and without a concrete belief system. From sporadic visits to temples and churches, the teachings, stories, and Scriptures were meaningless syllables bouncing off my ears.

An immigrant from Vietnam to a small business owner in America—I had made it. Consumed with pride, greed, and proud of the achievement, I unknowingly fed my innermost demons. Carefree decisions and addictions began to seize control. Content with my comfortable lifestyle, self-improvement was an afterthought.

On the brink of self-destruction upon facing sudden adversities, depleted stocks, and nearly losing my business, I was drenched with fears of losing my family. I was immersed in insidious depression, no answers, and no way out, and I selfishly turned to faith with a yearning cry for help. I had been absent from church for many years, but I gathered my shame and took my family and I discovered faith on a beautiful Easter morning.

My whole life abruptly changed when I accepted Christ and

embraced God. This led me to confessing sins and dark secrets to my wife, resulting in releasing the burdens and afflictions. I unveiled the courage to live again—to strive toward righteousness.

Significant changes occurred in every aspect of my life. I began *living* the words and not just *hearing* them. Faith replaced dismay and inadequacy. My conceit and stubbornness withered like leaves. I never imagined grasping a book and laying down my phone. I started journaling; meditations became prayers. I was disciplined with financial decisions, healthy eating, and embracing all music.

My speech and appearance underwent a drastic transformation as well. Anxiety perished, along with constraints of stress and worry. Freed from the web of negative energy, I blossomed from a larva of addictions. Though I quelled the fears and conquered myself, I acknowledged the evil spirit's presence that never rests. My spirit was healed and refined—an added soul to God's Kingdom.

My desire for forgiveness forged me forward. I found courage to ask forgiveness from those from whom I garnered hatred and envy, and who had sinned against me. I joined a church group, attended my first Bible study, and overcame the formidable coaching barriers by coaching my son's soccer team.

Separated from social media, self-indulgent entertainment, politics, and news, I became more sociable and sought meaningful friendships. Spending more time with my family was the true happiness I had overlooked and taken for granted. Time was cherished and no longer wasted.

On this path, faith manifested in me the unimaginable idea of writing a book, even though I had never read a single book in my adult life. I am now strengthened with the courage to pursue a meaningful life with God.

* * *

Andy Bui, who immigrated from Vietnam at the age of five, currently resides in Mississippi. He is a devoted husband, father, coach, small business owner, and writer with a rich cultural, and multiple religious, backgrounds.

Questions for Personal Reflection or Group Discussion

Andy Bui tells about being raised in a culturally and religiously mixed environment and growing up with a sense of spiritual confusion. Living a life marked by pride, he plunged into personal and professional disaster. One Easter morning becomes Andy's turning point. He connects with a deep faith in God, leading him to overcome past vices and embrace a new purpose.

Here are a few questions for personal reflection or group discussion:

1. Andy moves from a state of spiritual confusion and apathy to a profound personal transformation through faith. Reflect on your own spiritual journey or lack of one. What life moments have defined or changed your personal beliefs?
2. Ponder how challenges and hardships can sometimes lead to personal or spiritual growth. Have you experienced a similar transformation during times of difficulty? If so, please reflect upon it.
3. Andy asked for God's forgiveness and chose to forgive others. How did those steps prove crucial in his journey? How does the act of forgiveness bring well-being and mend relationships?

Made in the USA
Columbia, SC
28 May 2024